standard catalog of® 1950s CHEVROLET

Jon G. Robinson

©2006 Krause Publications
Published by

kp krause publications
An Imprint of F+W Publications

700 East State Street • Iola, WI 54990-0001
715-445-2214 • 888-457-2873

Our toll-free number to place an order or obtain
a free catalog is (800) 258-0929.

Library of Congress Catalog Number: 2006922204

ISBN 13-digit: 978-0-89689-177-7
ISBN 10-digit: 0-89689-177-1

Designed by Elizabeth Krogwold
Edited by Brian Earnest

Printed in China

CONTENTS

ACKNOWLEDGMENTS

(In the order in which I contacted them) Tom Meleo, information and introductions; Pinky Randall, information and introductions; Dennis and Jean Fink, publishers and editors of the *Generator and Distributor*, publication of the Vintage Chevrolet Club of America; Larry Pearson, information and '56 Bel Air sport sedan; Jim Malony, author *Bowties of the '50s*, information, and '58 Impala; Chap Morris Sr., William L. Morris Chevrolet, Fillmore, California, dealer memories; Bob McDorman, Bob McDorman Chevrolet, Canal Winchester, Ohio, photographs of his entire collection from the '50s; Jim Applegate, Applegate Chevrolet, Flint, Michigan, dealership memories and vintage photos; Steve Rosenberg, introductions; Juan Chavez, '54 Bel Air station wagon; Woody Stroope, '57 Bel Air sedan; Dan Hart and Paul Kander, '55 Bel Air convertible; Ted Taylor, '51 Deluxe sedan; Irv Kushner, '55 Nomad; Bill Quinn, '53 Bel Air hardtop; Kent McCombs, '51 Fleetline; John Murray, '52 Bel Air; Jerry Wassenburger, '54 Bel Air sedan; Jan Spradling, '50 Deluxe coupe; Manuel Rojas, '54 Bel Air convertible; Jerry Fulps, '56 Bel Air convertible; Dave Pouquette, Twisters/Route 66 Place, Williams, Arizona, '53 210 coupe; Alan Ricard, '53 210 coupe; Tim Futter, '57 150 sedan; Monte and Jo Hallertz, Chevyland USA Museum, Elm Creek, Nebraska, '55 Bel Air hardtop photo and '59 Impala hardtop factory photo; Harry Carter, Carter Country car sales, Lebanon, Oregon, '58 Biscayne sedan; Bill Dirnberger, research materials; Gene Clarey, '50 Deluxe two-door sedan, '52 Deluxe coupe; Ron Mandevill and Lucille Mandeville-Benoit, Mandeville Chevrolet, North Attleboro, Massachusetts, dealership memories; Dick Stowers, Culberson-Stowers Chevrolet, Pampa, Texas, Powerglide memories and introductions; Les Foss, retired from Whitney's Chevrolet, Montesano, Washington, dealership memories; Jerry Holz, Holz Motors, Hales Corners, Wisconsin, dealership memories; Fred Lossman, *Fingertip Facts* for the 1955 Chevrolet and '55 Bel Air two-door sedan; David Holt, 348 information; Charlie Reavis, Charlie Tranny, Michigan, Turboglide information; Martin Trouillon, Martin's Transmission Service, Los Angeles, California, Turboglide information; Dave Blanck, Blanck Chevrolet, Brownsburg, Indiana, dealership photos; Robert Davis, '56 Bel Air sport sedan; Frank North, Ferman Chevrolet, Tampa, Florida, dealership photos.

Special thanks to those who conducted photography: Dick Romm, Craig Murphy, Marc Mirabile and Fred Lossman

Photographic assistance: Doretta Kegel-Hill, David Hinckley.

A special thanks goes out to all the members and leadership of the Vintage Chevrolet Club of America. The photography in this book would not have been possible without them.

To all, thank you!

INTRODUCTION

*(Craig Murphy and
Jim Applegate Collection)*

Welcome to the *Standard Catalog of 1950s Chevrolet!* This year-by-year history of Chevrolet Motor Division features detailed descriptions of cars, features and personalities.

The Apology

Most encyclopedic books attempt to present the absolute facts, but in the swirling world of automobile production, the facts can be hard to come by, leaving the encyclopedia to confirm the unconfirmable. A car company invested millions of dollars into producing a line of automobiles, and decades later, there are nearly no records that the company even built the car. Previous editions in the *Standard Catalog* series deserve huge credit for the monumental task of establishing their first database of bare-bones information, and the information has been added to, corrected, and confirmed over the years.

Is every production figure perfect? Is every shipping weight perfect? No, but the proportions are.

Did a Chevrolet leave the factory with an option that wasn't on the options list? It wasn't uncommon.

Did a Chevrolet from one year have a trim piece that didn't exist until the following year? It's quite possible, if the car was built at the end of the model-year run.

Did cars come loaded with accessories that didn't belong on them? Yes, most often because the factories delivered more accessories than cars to the dealers at times.

The *Standard Catalogs* are not perfect, but they serve as reliable guides. They may not always hit the bullseye, but they always hit the target.

Chevrolet

William C. Durant was a hard-pushing, over-reaching business gambler who made and lost fortunes. He had made a tidy profit from his Durant-Dort carriage company, and he decided to get into the automobile game by buying Buick in 1904. Meanwhile, Benjamin Briscoe had made a fortune in the sheet metal industry, had owned Buick for a short time, and had been successful building cars with Jonathan Maxwell.

There are conflicting reports about the exact date, but right around 1905, Durant and Briscoe had the same idea at the same time. Both had determined there were too many car companies and that the whole industry would be better off if the companies were consolidated into a few large conglomerates instead of hundreds of small independents. Briscoe formed the United States Motor Company, and Durant formed General Motors. On the strength of Maxwell, Briscoe bought Stoddard-Dayton, Columbia, Brush, and several others. Durant's massive Buick profits acquired him Oldsmobile, Cadillac and other small car companies. Both Briscoe and Durant bought up various venders—companies supplying materials to the auto industry.

The competition between the United States Motor Company and General Motors was more about the two men's egos than it was about good business practices. Both companies broke under their frenzy to buy out other companies. The United States Motor Company lasted until 1913 when Briscoe turned for help to Walter Flanders, a maker of motorcycles and electric cars. Flanders dropped every company but Maxwell, and when Maxwell finally needed a revamp in the 1920s, it took on an experienced railroad man, engineer and former Buick manager who had just left Ford Motor Company. His name was Walter P. Chrysler.

Durant's General Motors didn't make it as far as the United States Motor Company and was in deep trouble by 1910, when a group of bankers took over the company and showed Durant to the door. Durant's ego couldn't take it, and he wanted GM back. While he owned Buick, he had become acquainted with a trio of French immigrant brothers who ran the Buick racing team among several other jobs they had with Buick—Louis, Gaston and Authur Chevrolet.

Louis Chevrolet was a world-famous racing driver and his name put Durant's new company on the map. Durant formed the Little Motor Car Company in 1911 and built a cute economy car, and he assigned Louis Chevrolet to design the larger, upscale car that would bear his name.

The Chevrolet Classic Six appeared in 1912. It was a big, luxurious high-quality car with a self-starter, speedometer, electric headlights, electric dash light, demountable rims, accessory spare wheel carriers, a 20-gallon fuel tank with gas gauge and 2-gallon auxiliary tank, and a running-board-mounted tool kit. Durant was back in the car business in a big way and, in 1913, two economy-class Chevrolets appeared wearing the names Light Six and four-cylinder Royal Mail. Durant was back in financial trouble by 1915 and lost General Motors for good.

Chevrolet made its last effort in the luxury class in 1918 with the Model D—a big, high-tech car with smooth lines, a comfortable interior, beautiful wood trim and an overhead-valve V-8 engine with nickel-plated valve covers that looked more like a Buick Century engine from the 1950s than anything else built in the 'teens.

The Model D didn't last long, and Chevrolet existed more as an economy make by the 1920s. Chevrolet was very successful with its model 490 into the first few years of the 1920s. Chevrolet made one more reach into technology with a disastrous air-cooled model called the Copper-Cooled Chevrolet. The Copper-Cooled Chevrolet was such a failure that it drove the president of the company to a nervous breakdown.

By the late 1920s, Ford had been number one with the rickety but reliable Model T for nearly 20 years. The Model T was outdated by 1915, but Ford nursed the Model T through most of the Jazz Age until finally relenting to competitive pressure from Chevrolet with the introduction of the four-cylinder Model A in 1928. Chevrolet was ready for the Model A with a six-cylinder engine that would take the bowtie into the 1950s and beyond in varying forms. The six was introduced in 1929, and its cast-iron pistons and obtrusive head bolts earned it the affectionate nickname "stovebolt six."

In the 1930s and '40s, Chevrolet handily outsold both of its main competitors, Ford and Plymouth, although the former had a V-8 and the latter had a reputation for outstanding engineering.

William Holler was Chevrolet's secret weapon. Holler was the company's head of sales through the 1930s, and he put strict requirements on Chevrolet dealers to serve their customers and communities. This program cemented customer loyalty so strongly that Chevrolet beat its two biggest competitors all the way through the 1960s.

With World War II over and growing postwar prosperity, the United States was in a state of calm excitement as the 1950s approached. Finally, after 15 miserable years, Americans could look forward to their individual futures instead of their next meal, and the auto industry was ready to deliver fantastic new machines for the new superhighways.

General Motors conceived Futuramic bodies for Oldsmobiles in 1948. Chevrolet got the new bodies in 1949, and the stage was set for an era that would be remembered warmly for optimistic modernity and America at its best.

The 1950s

The 1950s began in the Jet Age and ended in the Space Age, with all of it reflected in the cars. American cars entered the 1950s with round tail lights that imitated jet engines and left the 1950s with push-button dashboards and leaning radio antennas that imitated Sputnik. They entered the 1950s with aviation streamlining and left the 1950s with space-rocket streamlining. They began the decade with quietly elegant, neutrally colored cloth interiors, and they ended it with colorful, fashionable interiors influenced by the colors and fabrics that were popular at the Paris fashion shows.

In spite of their Jet Age looks, Chevrolets were still in the early-1930s mechanically in 1950 with splash-oiled engines, babbitt engine bearings, and enclosed driveshafts. Fords and Plymouths were more up to date, but Chevrolet's dominance of the marketplace was so strong that, by the end of the decade, the federal government was watching General Motors for anti-trust law violations.

The 1950s had a downside, however, at least to the modern day car lover. Nothing was more important socially than being modern, and the throw-away car culture set in. Cars improved so quickly between 1900 and 1940 that if a guy traded in an older car for a newer one, he really was getting a better car, and there really were good reasons for buying a new car from time to time. By the 1950s, having an older car just became a fashion-based embarrassment for many people, and they threw away good cars quickly.

On the other hand, a compilation of automotive reliability statistics from 1957 shows that automotive reliability increased tremendously from 1930 to 1940, but between 1946 and 1953 reliability decreased noticeably. Engines and electrical systems were the biggest culprits. All economy-class cars in the early-

1950s still had engines from the 1930s, but they were doing a 1950s job on the new freeways.

After Chevrolet improved the six-cylinder cars with full-pressure engine oiling, insert bearings and much improved rear axle ratios in 1953, there was no longer a good reason to throw away a Chevrolet except fashion. This became even more true after the V-8 introduction in 1955, but optimistic modernity carried the day.

The 1950s were optimistic, and the cars were optimistic. Teenagers could gather in large numbers without the boys fighting or the girls getting "in trouble." The teenagers of that time grew up through the tumult of the 1960s, the gas crunch of the 1970s, and the sad state of American cars in the 1980s. They missed the cars of their youth.

Cars from the 1950s remind Americans of their country at its best. The cars were not just transportation. They were color television, chrome kitchens and hi-fi. They were Dave Brubeck, Truman Capote and *Playhouse 90*. They showed the world that a free American man who grew up in the Depression and got shot at in the war could give his family a new house and two cars on one income. They portrayed freedom and optimism on wheels, and Chevrolet put in all within the reach of a low-income guy.

The *Standard Catalog* series puts authoritative automotive information and history within the reach of the low-income guy, too. With information comes confidence, and hopefully, the information and history in the *Standard Catalog of 1950s Chevrolet* will help someone who wants to preserve a Chevrolet in its original condition decide which Chevrolet to get and understand what part it plays in the Jet Age, Space Age and 21st century.

CHAPTER 1

The 1950s began with Chevrolet nicely face-lifting the 1949 models. The '49s have a row of little teeth in the bottom-most slot in the grille opening, but in 1950, there were only the two ribbed pillars under the parking lights. The 1950 dash was also a carryover from 1949, and on Deluxe models, it was smartly two-toned. Chevrolet gave a more luxurious feel to its economy class cars than its competition.

1950

Introduction World War II had been over for nearly five years, the waiting lists for new cars were gone. America was optimistic and Chevrolet was ready for a new decade.

The 1950 Chevrolet's styling ancestor is the 1948 Oldsmobile Futuramic 98—a sleeker, lower, cleaner, less bulging car that announced loudly that the prewar world was gone. Oldsmobile's successful new breed of car spread throughout the 1949 GM lineup. As applied to Chevrolet, the Futuramic styling promised a new world of transportation for the car buyer of modest means.

The 1950 models changed little from 1949. The '49 grille had a row of thin teeth in its lower jaw, but the teeth disappeared in 1950. This left only a single ribbed pillar under each protruding parking light. The 1950 hood badge was bigger than the '49 had been and its wings pointed slightly down instead of angling upwards as in 1949. The list of features included: combined taillights and brake lights, bright rocker moldings, black rubber rear fender gravel shields, dual license plate lights, single-control dual windshield wipers, a rugged frame, an improved suspension with diagonally mounted airplane-type shock absorbers, sound-absorbing roof insulation, foam rubber seat cushions, extra-low-pressure tires, a Hand-E-Gearshift transmission control, push-button starting, Certi-Safe hydraulic brakes, extra-wide (5-ft.-wide) seats, lightweight pistons, torque-tube drive with a fully enclosed tubular propeller shaft, open-type Knee-Action front suspension, stainless-steel body moldings and Venti-Panes (GM's name for vent windows).

Chevrolet introduced Powerglide automatic transmission, describing it as "a complete no-shift driving system with a special engine and Economizer rear axle."

The entry-level line was called the Special series and the top-level line was the Deluxe series. Both had Styleline (notch back) and Fleetline (fastback) body styles in them. There were nine distinct body types, with convertibles and station wagons offered only in the Deluxe series. The full car line added up to 14 models.

I.D. NUMBERS: Serial numbers were stamped on a plate on the left front door hinge pillar. Engine numbers were stamped on the right side of the block near the fuel pump. The first symbol in the serial number indicated assembly plant as follows: (1) Flint, Michigan, (2) Tarrytown, New York, (3) St. Louis, Missouri, (5) Kansas City, Missouri, (6) Oakland, California, (8) Atlanta, Georgia, (9) Norwood, Ohio, (14) Baltimore, Maryland, (20) Los Angeles, California, (21) Janesville, Wisconsin. The second symbol indicated the model year: H=1950. The third symbol indicated the model and series: J=Special 1500 series, K=Deluxe 2100 series. The fourth symbol indicates the month of manufacture: A=January, etc. The remaining symbols are the production sequence number in the specific factory. Serial numbers for Michigan-built 1950 Specials were: HJ-1001 to 49801. Engine numbers were: HA-1001 to 1320152. Serial numbers for Michigan-built 1950 Deluxes were: HK-1001 to 187118. Deluxe engine numbers fit into the same sequence listed for Special Series above. The Fisher Body number plate on the right-hand side of the cowl gives additional information, such as the Body Style Number (see second column in tables below), the body production sequence number, the trim (upholstery) number code and the paint number code.

PAINT COLORS: Monotone paint colors for 1950 were: No. 423 Mayland Black, No. 424 Oxford Maroon, No. 425 Grecian Gray, No. 426 Crystal Green, No. 427 Falcon Gray, No. 428 Windsor Blue, No. 429 Mist Green, No. 430 Rodeo Beige, No. 431 Moonlite Cream and No. 437 Grecian Gray. Two-tone paint combinations for 1950 were No. 432 Falcon Gray/Grecian Gray, No. 433 Crystal Green/Mist Green, No. 434 Maryland Black/Mist Green, No. 435 Grecian Gray/Windsor Blue and No. 436 Falcon Gray/Moonlight Cream.

SPECIAL SERIES—SIX-CYL—1500 HJ : The Special series was the price leader for the new decade and these cars wore almost no body trim. Styleline Specials had bustle back styling. Fleetline Specials had sweeping fastback lines. Drivers looked through a curved windshield with black rubber moldings and a chrome center strip. The upholstery was gray-striped modern weave flat cloth with dark gray broadcloth and plain, light gray door panels. Light gray control knobs replaced the ivory-type used in 1949. Black rubber floor mats were used in the front passenger compartment with carpet found in the rear of sedans and coupes.

SPECIAL SERIES 1500 HJ

STYLELINE SUB-SERIES

Model No.	Body/Style No.	Body Type & Seating	Factory Price	Shipping Weight	Production Total
1503	1269	4d Sed-6P	$1,450	3,120 lbs.	55,644
1502	1211	2d Sed-6P	$1,403	3,085 lbs.	89,897
1524	1227	2d Spt Cpe-6P	$1,408	3,050 lbs.	28,328
1504	1227B	2d Bus Cpe-3P	$1,329	3,025 lbs.	20,984

FLEETLINE SUB-SERIES

1553	1208	4d Sed-6P	$1,450	3,115 lbs.	23,277
1552	1207	2d Sed-6P	$1,403	3,080 lbs.	43,682

NOTE 1: *Fisher Body/Style Numbers: First two symbols in main number identify series (12=Special). Second two symbols in main number identify body type (69=four-door sedan, 11=two-door sedan, etc.). All style numbers are proceeded by the last two digits of model year and a hyphen. The style number is located on vehicle data plate under hood and is the best way to positively identify Chevrolet body styles.*

DELUXE SERIES—SIX-CYL—2100 HK : In addition to all features found on Specials, the Deluxe had its model name on the front fenders, stainless-steel windshield moldings, a body trim spear running down each front fender and on to the front doors, bright side window frames, a fancier two-spoke steering wheel, two sun visors, carpeted front floor mat inserts and two-tone tan-and-brown dashboard finish. Rear fender skirts were common on Deluxe models. Styleline Deluxes were notchback cars and Fleetline Deluxes were fastbacks, just as in the Special line.

Deluxe interiors were trimmed with gray striped broadcloth material. This model had "off-shoulder" dark gray broadcloth contrast panels and dark gray front seatback cushions, seat risers, door panels and center pillars, along with a light gray headliner.

The new Bel Air sport coupe (two-door hardtop) had a three-piece wraparound curved back window. The Bel Air sport coupe used the convertible body, doors and windshield with an attractive metal roof grafted on. The sport coupe roof had no center pillar. With the windows rolled down, it gave the airy feeling of a convertible, but its hardtop offered the protected feeling of a closed car. The Bel Air's interior features are the same as in the convertible, except for two rear compartment lights at roof quarter panels, a neutral gray headliner with chrome roof bows and a black plastic gearshift knob. The interior rearview mirrors sat down low on the dashboard on Bel Air sport coupes and convertibles, so drivers could see through their much lower rear windows.

Powerglide-equipped cars announced the presence of the optional automatic transmission on the stylized trunk handle. Since the Powerglide cars had a bigger engine with pressurized oiling, they also had a higher-capacity oil pressure gauge in the dashboard.

DELUXE SERIES 2100 HK

STYLELINE SUB-SERIES

Model No.	Body/Style No.	Body Type & Seating	Factory Price	Shipping Weight	Production Total
2103	1069	4d Sed-6P	$1,529	3,150 lbs.	316,412
2102	1011	2d Sed-6P	$1,482	3,100 lbs.	248,567
2124	1027	2d Spt Cpe-6P	$1,498	3,090 lbs.	81,536
2154	1037	2d Bel Air-6P	$1,741	3,225 lbs.	76,662
2134	1067	2d Conv-5P	$1,847	3,380 lbs.	32,810
2119	1062	4d Sta Wag-8P	$1,994	3,460 lbs.	166,995

FLEETLINE SUB-SERIES

Model No.	Body/Style No.	Body Type & Seating	Factory Price	Shipping Weight	Production Total
2153	1008	4d Sed-6P	$1,529	3145 lbs.	124,287
2152	1007	2d Sed-6P	$1,482	3115 lbs.	189,509

NOTE 1: *Style Number 1037 is a two-door pillarless hardtop sport coupe.*

ENGINES:

ALL SERIES SIX-CYLINDER: Overhead-valve. Cast-iron block. Displacement: 216.5 cid. Bore and stroke: 3 ½ x 3 ¾ in. Compression ratio: 6.5:1. Brake hp: 90 at 3300 rpm. Four main bearings. Solid valve lifters. Carburetor: Rochester one-barrel 7002050. Cooling capacity: 15 qt. Crankcase capacity: 5.5 qt. without filter.

CHASSIS: Box girder frame. In convertible a "VK" structure of I-beam members took the place of engine rear support cross member. Open Knee-Action front suspension with direct, double-acting shock absorbers. Ride stabilizer. Rubber insulated semi-elliptic rear springs with metal covers. Direct double-acting hydraulic rear shock absorbers. Four-wheel hydraulic brakes with 11-in. drums. Wheelbase: (all) 115 in. Overall length: (passenger car) 197 ½ in., (station wagon) 198 ¼ in. Width: 73 ¹⁵/₁₆ in. Height: 65 ¾ in. Front tread: (all) 57 in. Rear tread: (all) 58 ¾ in. Rear axle: Semi-floating with hypoid drive and 4.11:1 gear ratio. Torque tube drive with tubular propeller shaft, both fully enclosed. Tires: 6.70 x 15 blackwall on wide-base rims. Six-volt electrical system. Gas tank capacity: 16 gal.

OPTIONS: Powerglide two-speed automatic transmission was introduced as a $159 option for Deluxe series only. Cars so equipped were provided with a modified Chevrolet truck engine with 3 ⁹/₁₆ x 3 ¹⁵/₁₆ in. bore and stroke and 235 cid of piston displacement. Hydraulic valve lifters and larger intake valves were used. Horsepower was rated the familiar 90 at 3300 rpm. Powerglide-equipped cars had 3.55:1 rear axle gear ratio. Also, 7.10 x 15 tires ($14.75 extra) were optional for convertibles equipped with Powerglide. Standard manual radio. Deluxe push-button radio. Radio antenna. Under-dash heater and defroster. In-dash Deluxe heater and defroster. White sidewall tires. Wheel trim rings. Spotlight. Fog lights. Directional signals. Back-up light. External windshield sun shade (visor). Tan, striped pattern, free-breathing pile fabric Deluxe series upholstery trim. San-Toy seat covers. Outer bumper tips. Master grille guard. Locking gas filler cap. Other standard factory and/or dealer installed accessories.

HISTORICAL FOOTNOTES: Dealer introduction was January 7, 1950. Model-year production was 1,371,535 units. Calendar-year sales totaled 1,520,577. Chevrolet is America's number one automaker again. Bel Air Sport Coupe introduced. Powerglide automatic transmission introduced. Hydraulic valve lifters adopted for Powerglide six-cylinder engine. New Rochester carburetor was B- or BC-type ("C" indicating automatic choke). Some cars also had Stromberg BXVD-2 or BXXD-35 carburetors.

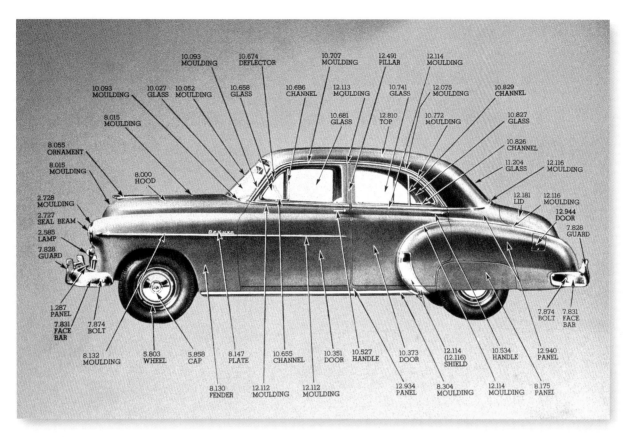

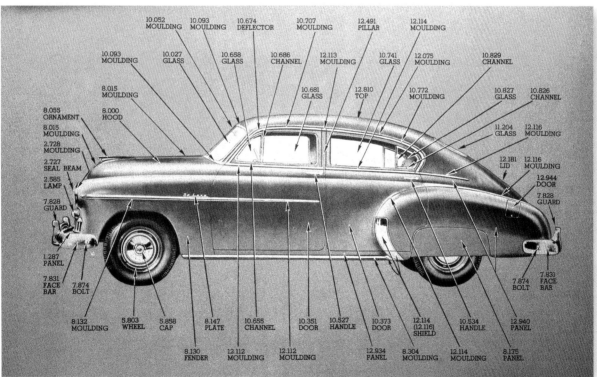

General Motors' technical rendition of the beginning of the 1950s showing the fastback Fleetline and the notchback Styleline bodies. The Fleetlines were sleek, smooth, and in keeping with the Jet Age, but at the time, fastbacks were rapidly becoming relics of the 1940s, and the Styleline was the more modern-seeming car in 1950. (Bill Dirberger collection)

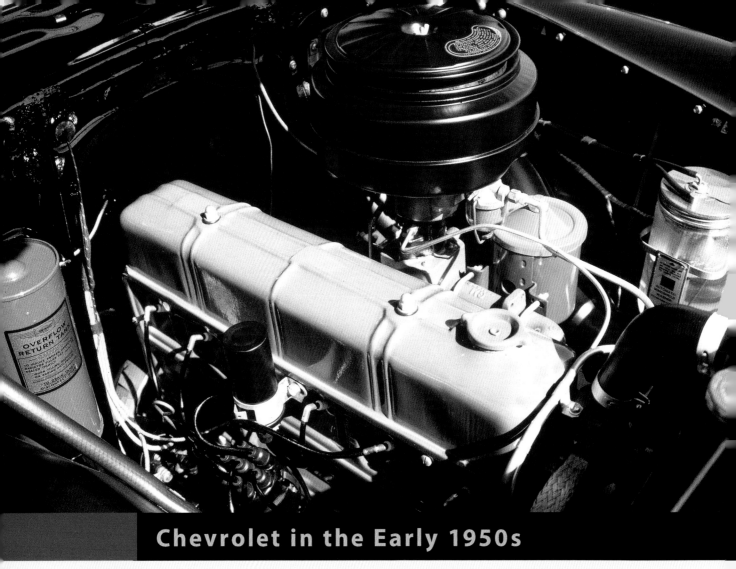

Chevrolet in the Early 1950s

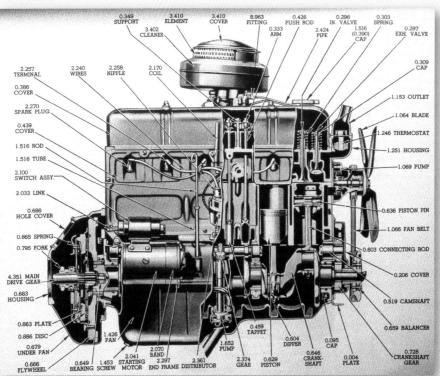

The venerable Chevrolet six entered the 1950s as an old-fashioned engine from the 1930s with splash-oiling and babbit bearings, but it had a solid reputation a was quite reliable if the driver drove wi the engine's limitations. It outsold the pressure-oiled, insert-bearing Plymout two-to-one and outsold Ford's V-8 by a substantial margin. A Chevrolet could be ordered with the optional Powerglic transmission in 1950, and with Powerg a Chevrolet car had the same pressure-insert-bearing, 235-cubic-inch six foun GMC trucks. Powerglide models also ha much better rear axle ratio that revved engine 15 percent slower than a manu shift Chevrolet.

(Bill Dirnberger collection)

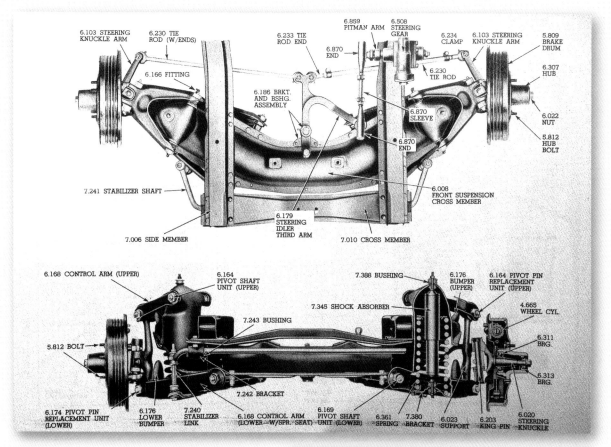

Chevrolet wasn't completely behind the times, and improvements to suspension with "aircraft-style" shock absorbers and Jumbo-Drum brakes helped the cars drive better and have a more modern feel. The aircraft shocks were also maintenance-free compared to the old-fashioned dual-action shocks.

(Bill Dirberger collection)

The '50 Chevy was basically a '30s car in '50s clothing. It was an "old-tech" car with its splash engine oiling, torque-tube drive and other old-fashioned features.

The Chevrolet engine was reliable and durable, if shown proper care. Clean oil was a must. Moderate driving speeds were recommended. But if taken care of, the Chevrolet six held together well. In those days, motorists did a lot more periodic maintenance at home, so the "Stovebolt Six" made many friends who became loyal Chevrolet buyers.

Even Chevrolet loyalists sometimes called the splash system "dip-and-hope" oiling. The oil pump generated just 15 lbs. or so of pressure. Six little nozzles pointed at the bearing caps and squirted oil on them as they swept around at the bottom of the piston stroke. The nozzles filled a trough for each bearing. "Dippers" on the bearing caps passed through the oil-filled troughs and the streams of oil from the nozzles.

The 1951 Fleetline fastback sedan has the cozy feel of the 1930s and '40s combined with a sleek Jet Age shape, but the 1952 Bel Air hardtop has the sunny, optimistic, open-air feeling of the 1950s.

1951 Fleetline fastback

The Chevrolet rod bearings were actually part of the rods. They were made of a soft, replaceable material called *babbit*. When the bearings wore out, the machinist melted the old babbit out of the connecting rod, poured new babbit into it and then machined the bearing to size.

Chevrolet's enclosed driveshaft was another throwback to the past. This design eliminated any possibility of Chevrolet conveniently or cost-effectively offering an optional overdrive transmission. Still, the Chevrolet had a reputation for good fuel mileage, so the lack of an overdrive didn't hurt its sales very much.

For Chevrolet fans, 1950 brought three pieces of good news. The first was the introduction of Chevrolet's first two-door hardtop—the Bel Air. The higher-priced GM cars had offered this body style earlier, but for Chevrolet buyers, the new body style was worth the wait. It had the same convertible-like roofline as its more expensive GM siblings, but it looked more nimble with its smaller wheelbase.

The second big news item of 1950 was the

introduction of Chevrolet's first optional automatic transmission—the cast-iron two-speed Powerglide. When a 1950 Chevrolet was ordered with Powerglide, it came with a bigger and more advanced 235-cid six that featured full-pressure oiling and insert bearings. Powerglide cars used a rear axle ratio that lowered the engine rpms by 15 percent. With the "235," the Chevy became a faster highway cruiser that no longer held up traffic.

The third piece of news to come out of Chevrolet headquarters in Flint, Michigan, was that the company's 1950 model outsold Plymouth 2 to 1 and Ford by a substantial margin. This kind of success proved that Chevrolet had it over the competition when it came to looks. Chevrolet's one-year-old body was little changed and reflected the same aircraft-inspired Jet Age styling it introduced in 1949. Plymouths and Fords were also redesigned in 1949, but the Ford looked like a shoebox and the Plymouth looked like a box on a box.

Chevrolets were merchandised in two series. The Special 1500 was the lower-priced line and the cars had

door business coupe made up the Styleline offerings. In the Deluxe 2100 series, the offerings included two- and four-door sedans, a sport coupe, the Bel Air two-door hardtop, a five-passenger convertible and a four-door station wagon.

The rapidly aging Fleetline fastbacks were graceful. Compared to the "turtle-back" fastbacks that Dodge and Plymouth were offering in their low-priced lines, the Fleetline looked like a rocket. Ford had no fastback model, but it was actually the fastest of the three with a top speed of 90 mph. The average top speed for a 1950 Chevrolet with manual shift, as reported in the September 1950 issue of *Motor Trend*, was 85.55 mph. In its April 1952 issue, the same magazine printed the top speed of both 1950 and 1952 Plymouths. For the earlier car with a 3.9.0:1 rear axle, the number was 80.30 mph. Due to its gearing, the Plymouth was actually faster than the stick-shifted Chevy from 0 to 60 mph. However, with the optional Powerglide automatic transmission, the Chevrolet would keep up nicely with a Ford and its speed was a better match for its styling.

Times were changing quickly, and in 1951, Chevrolet got a new simpler grille with arrow-shaped parking lights and a more modern dash. Powerglide became even more popular, and little by little, the driving public found out the Powerglide rear end would retrofit into earlier manual-shift Chevrolets and make them much more capable on the highway. The Deluxe interiors were available in a wider array of colors, and it was becoming easier to personalize cars even in the low-price range.

The 1951 rear fenders were crowned a little higher than they had been in 1950, and slowly, the car was morphing into something that looked less like a 1940s car. In 1952, Chevrolet produced only a small number of fastback Fleetlines, and the 1940s were finally over. Looking back now, the Fleetlines seem so sleek and aerodynamic, and they seem in keeping with the era's Jet Age imagery, but at the time, they belonged in the 1940s. The 1950s looked forward with lots of glass and open-air hardtops—cars that looked like convertibles even when they weren't. In the 1930s and '40s, closed cars had a closed look. Sedans looked cozy and protected in the '40s, but in the 1950s, customers wanted the open, optimistic, airy, sunny, light-colored cars that reflected the mood of the times, and the closed, dark-colored cars of the '40s suddenly looked like prisons.

With the end of the 1952 run, Chevrolet drivetrains were finally out of the 1930s, and with the death of the Fleetline, Chevrolet bodies were leaving the 1940s, but the best was yet to come. Even the most decked-out 1952 Bel Air hardtop would be old-fashioned in a heartbeat.

less window dressing. No body side trim was used on these models. They had black rubber rear fender gravel guards. Inside was a Spartan interior. The Deluxe 2100 series offered buyers a one-step-up car. The 2100s had bright metal body moldings and gravel guards outside, plus nicer upholstery inside.

Each series offered Fleetline (fastback) two- and four-door sedans and Styleline (notch back) models of varying body styles. In the Special 1500 series, two- and four-door sedans, a two-door sport coupe and a two-

Even GM's lowest-priced cars were getting more colorful interiors in the early 1950s. On Bel Air hardtops, the rear window had a low field of vision and the rearview mirror had to be mounted lower and nearly rested on top of the dash.

The 1951 and 1952 Chevrolets can be a little hard to tell apart, but it's easy if you know the tricks. The '51 grille has a smooth center bar, and the '52 has teeth. The '51 parking light is smaller and has decorative slots in the housing, and the '52 parking light lens is larger and has no slots. This 1952 Bel Air has a rose-colored parking light, which some enthusiasts claim to have been a Chevrolet accessory at the time.

The 1951 announcement day at Applegate Chevrolet in Flint, Michigan.

(Jim Applegate collection)

CHAPTER 2

The gazelle hood ornament was an accessory for the 1951 Chevrolet.

1951

Introduction Chevrolet cleaned up the grille even more in 1951, leaving only a single bar running across the chrome-trimmed, somewhat rectangular grille opening. It was a subtle but attractive facelift. Moving the parking lamps into the lower grille opening under the headlamps made for a wider look.

First

in smooth, low-cost, No-Shift Driving

Yes, you'll enjoy the finest kind of *no-shift driving* at lowest cost—without clutch pedal, gearshift lever or gearshifting—with Chevrolet's exclusive Powerglide Automatic Transmission teamed with a 105-h.p. Valve-in-Head Engine!* Or the finest kind of *standard driving* at lowest cost with Chevrolet's world-famous Silent Synchro-Mesh Transmission teamed with the highly improved, more powerful standard Valve-in-Head engine! Choose a Chevrolet with either of these two great engines and drives and experience results exclusive to this one low-priced car!

*Combination of Powerglide Automatic Transmission and 105-h.p. Engine optional on De Luxe models at extra cost.

and Finest

for performance that's both thrilling and thrifty

City streets—modern highways—dirt or gravel roads, hills or mountains—all are easy for the Chevrolet owner. This car is designed and built to ride comfortably over all types of roads . . . to perform superlatively well in all seasons . . . and to continue to serve faithfully over a long period of years with surprisingly low cost for gas, oil and upkeep. Its abilities are proved; it brings you its own special combination of performance and economy; and, consequently, more people buy Chevrolets than any other make of car, year after year.

The Styleline De Luxe 4-Door Sedan

at Lowest Cost

with all these advantages for the least money

The most satisfying and gratifying thing of all is that Chevrolet offers so many features of highest-priced cars and yet remains the *lowest-priced line* of full-length cars in America. Features like Body by Fisher for outstanding beauty, comfort and safety . . . extra-wide "five-foot seats," the famous Unitized Knee-Action Ride and airplane-type shock absorbers for luxurious riding-ease . . . and Curved Windshield with Panoramic Visibility and Proved Certi-Safe Hydraulic Brakes for maximum safety-protection. See it—test it—and you will choose Chevrolet—*first and finest at lowest cost.*

AMERICA'S BEST SELLER . . . AMERICA'S BEST BUY

CHEVROLET MOTOR DIVISION, *General Motors Corporation*, DETROIT 2, MICHIGAN

44

Telling 1951 and 1952 models apart can be a challenge, but parking lights hold the key to identification. While both years' parking lights are arrow-shaped, the 1951 lens is smaller, and there is a row of vertical slots in the chrome housing inboard from the lens, whereas the 1952 lenses are much larger, more triangular and have no slots.

Once again, Fleetlines had fastback bodies, and Stylelines had notchback bodies.

Chevrolets still only came with one of two six-cylinder engines. The more technologically advanced 235 graced those cars equipped with Powerglide. Starting in 1951, Chevrolet also adopted new "Jumbo-Drum" brakes that had 15 percent more lining area and required 25 percent less pedal pressure. A curved "Safety-Light" instrument panel had all instruments compactly grouped in two clusters and lighting that eliminated glare. Other features included rivetless brake linings, "Reflector-Guard" tail lights, more storage space, torque-tube drive, a sealed exhaust system, a "Tip-Toe" clutch (with manual transmission), open-type Knee-Action, airplane-type shock absorbers, low-pressure tires, foam rubber seats and curved two-piece windshields.

I.D. NUMBERS: Serial numbers were stamped on a plate on the left front door hinge pillar. Engine numbers were stamped on the right side of the block near the fuel pump. The first symbol in the serial number indicated assembly plant as follows: (1) Flint, Michigan, (2) Tarrytown, New York, (3) St. Louis, Missouri, (5) Kansas City, Missouri, (6) Oakland, California, (8) Atlanta, Georgia, (9) Norwood, Ohio, (14) Baltimore, Maryland, (20) Los Angeles, California, (21) Janesville, Wisconsin. The second symbol indicated the model year: J=1951. The third symbol indicated the model and series: J=Special 1500 Series, K=Deluxe 2100 Series. The fourth symbol indicates the month of manufacture: A=January, etc. The last four symbols are the production sequence number in the specific factory. Serial numbers for Michigan-built 1951 Specials were: JJ-1001 to 32061, engine numbers were: JA-1001 to 1261301. Serial numbers for Michigan-built 1951 Deluxes were: JK-1001 to 174408. Deluxe engine numbers fit into same sequence listed for Special Series above. The Fisher Body number plate on the right-hand side of the cowl gives additional information, such as the body style number (see second column in tables below), the body production sequence number, the trim (upholstery) number code and the paint number code.

The sporty Bel Air hardtops were gaining in popularity, but the solid four-door sedan was always Chevrolet's most popular body style in the 1950s.

PAINT COLORS: Monotone paint colors for 1951 were: No. 442 Maryland Black, No. 443 Burgundy Red, No. 444 Thistle Gray, No. 445 Fathom Green, No. 446 Shadow Gray, No. 447 Trophy Blue, No. 448 Aspen Green, No. 449 Aztec Tan and No. 450 Moonlight Cream. Two-tone paint combinations for 1951 were: No. 451 Shadow Gray/Thistle Gray, No. 452 Fathom Green/Aspen Green, No. 453 Maryland Black/Moonlight Cream, No. 454 Thistle Gray/Trophy Blue, No. 455 Thistle Gray/Shadow Gray, No. 456 Aspen Green/Fathom Green, No. 460 Shadow Gray Poly/Thistle Gray, No. 461 Thistle Gray/Shadow Gray Poly, No. 464 Fathom Green/Aspen Green and No. 465 Aspen Green/Fathom Green.

SPECIAL SERIES—SIX-CYL—1500 JJ: Styleline Specials had bustle backs and no chrome body strip. Fleetline Specials had fastbacks and no chrome body strip. Black rubber mudguards were seen on both Special lines. Two-tone gray interiors with light-gray striped pattern cloth upholstery were used. Equipment features followed the 1949-1950 assortment. Tail lights were smaller with nearly square red plastic lenses, and they carried a small, round reflector at the bottom of the tail light housing. Specials still came only with the base engine and standard transmission.

The 1951 Chevrolet grille had no teeth. The parking lights were arrow-shaped and decorated with slotted chrome bezels.

SPECIAL SERIES 1500 JJ

STYLELINE SUB-SERIES

Model No.	Body/Style No.	Body Type & Seating	Factory Price	Shipping Weight	Production Total
1503	1269	4d Sed-6P	$1,594	3,110 lbs.	63,718
1502	1211	2d Sed-6P	$1,540	3,070 lbs.	75,566
1524	1227	2d Spt Cpe-6P	$1,545	3,060 lbs.	18,981
1504	1227B	2d Bus Cpe-3P	$1,460	3,040 lbs.	17,020

FLEETLINE SUB-SERIES

Model No.	Body/Style No.	Body Type & Seating	Factory Price	Shipping Weight	Production Total
1553	1208	4d Sed-6P	$1,594	3,130 lbs.	3,364
1552	1207	2d Sed-6P	$1,540	3,090 lbs.	6,441

DELUXE SERIES—SIX-CYL—2100 JK: Deluxe models also used the newly designed grille that had the lower two horizontal bars extended to form a circular frame for oblong parking lamps with five vertical sectioned bars beside the parking lamps. Chevrolet script appeared on the chrome grille frame molding. Deluxes had a stainless-steel molding starting above the front wheel openings and extending onto doors with Deluxe nameplates integrated into them and bright-metal windshield moldings. Chrome rear fender gravel shields and painted fender skirts were standard equipment. Interiors were two-tone gray with gray striped broadcloth upholstery. Four different, special two-tone combinations were offered for Bel Air interiors. Bel Air upholstery was in two-tone gray striped pilecord fabric with buff leather bolsters. Station wagons were trimmed with tan imitation pigskin.

The young man on a budget who wanted a sporty look could do well buying the Fleetline two-door fastback in 1951, and he could load it up with fancy accessories.

A Powerglide-equipped car announced its presence in the stylized trunk handle, and because the Powerglide cars had the bigger engine with pressurized oiling, they also had a higher-capacity oil pressure gauge in the dash.

The interior rearview mirrors sat down low on the dashboard on Bel Air hardtops and convertibles so the driver could see through the much lower rear window. The cars carried a two-spoke steering wheel.

DELUXE SERIES I.D. NUMBERS: The numbers followed the same general system with new 'JK' alphabetical code. Serial numbers were JK-1001 to 174408. Engine numbers fit into the same sequence listed for Special Series above.

Chevrolets with manual transmissions carried the splash-oiled 216 cubic-inch overhead-valve six.

In spite of the rocket-shaped body, the Fleetline's dark, cozy 1940s feel was quickly being replaced by the light, airy feel of the Bel Air hardtop for the sporty-car buyer. The General Motors fastback was one of the defining cars of the Jet Age, and the Chevrolet Fleetline brought it to economy-car class.

While the fastback Fleetlines gave the buyer the sporty rocket-ship feel, the notchback Styline sedan gave the buyer the luxury-car feel and looked more like a Buick or Cadillac from the back. The notchback syling also complete more directly with Ford and Plymouth styling.

DELUXE SERIES 1500 JK

STYLELINE SUB-SERIES

Model No.	Body/Style No.	Body Type & Seating	Factory Price	Shipping Weight	Production Total
2103	1069	4d Sed-6P	$1,680	3,150 lbs.	380,270
2102	1011	2d Sed-6P	$1,629	3,110 lbs.	262,933
2124	1027	2d Spt Cpe-6P	$1,647	3,090 lbs.	64,976
2154	1037	2d Bel Air-6P	$1,914	3,215 lbs.	103,356
2134	1067	2d Conv-5P	$2,030	3,360 lbs.	20,172
2119	1062	4d Sta Wag-8P	$2,191	3,450 lbs.	23,586

FLEETLINE SUB-SERIES

Model No.	Body/Style No.	Body Type & Seating	Factory Price	Shipping Weight	Production Total
2153	1008	4d Sed-6P	$1,680	3,155 lbs.	57,693
2152	1007	2d Sed-6P	$1,629	3,125 lbs.	131,910

NOTE: *Style number 1037 is a two-door pillarless hardtop coupe.*

ENGINES:

ALL SERIES STANDARD SIX-CYL (MANUAL TRANSMISSION): Overhead-valve. Cast-iron block. Displacement: 216.5 cid. Bore and stroke: 3 ½ x 3 ¾ in. Compression ratio: 6.6:1. Brake hp: 92 at 3400 rpm. Four main bearings. Splash oiling. Solid valve lifters. Carburetor: Single-barrel Rochester, Carter and Stromberg models used in mixed production. Cooling system capacity: 15 qt. Crankcase capacity (less filter): 5.5 qt.

ALL SERIES STANDARD SIX-CYL (POWERGLIDE TRANSMISSION): Inline six. Overhead-valve. Cast-iron block. Displacement: 235.5 cid. Bore and stroke: 3 $^9/_{16}$ x 3 $^{15}/_{16}$ in. Four main bearings. Pressurized oiling. Hydraulic valve lifters. Compression ratio: 6.7:1. Brake hp: 105 at 3600 rpm. Carburetor: Rochester one-barrel BC. Cooling system capacity: 15 qt. Crankcase capacity less filter: 5.5 qt.

CHASSIS: Box girder frame. In the convertible, a "VK" structure of I-beam members took the place of engine rear support cross member. Open-type Knee-Action front suspension with direct double-acting shock absorbers. Ride stabilizer. Rubber insulated semi-elliptic rear springs with metal covers. Direct double-acting hydraulic rear shock absorbers. Four-wheel hydraulic brakes with 11-in. drums. Wheelbase: (all) 115 in. Overall length: (passenger cars) 197.75 in., (station wagon) 198 ⅞ in. Front tread: (all) 57 in. Rear tread: (all) 58 ¾ in. Rear axle: Semi-floating with hypoid drive and 4.11:1 gear ratio. Torque tube drive with tubular propeller shaft, both fully enclosed. Tires: 6.70 x 15 blackwall on wide-base rims, 7.10 x 15 on convertible. Gas tank capacity: 16 gal. 6-volt electrical system.

OPTIONS: Directional signals. Dash panel ashtray (standard in Deluxe). Manual radio. Deluxe push-button radio. Under-dash heater and defroster. Deluxe in-dash heater and defroster. Full wheel discs. Wheel trim rings. Whitewall tires. Thirty-nine-hour stem wind clock (standard in Deluxe). Fender skirts (standard on Deluxe). No-Mar Fuel door guard. Door handle shields. Front and rear bumper wing tips. Master grille guard. Spotlight. Fog lamps. External sun shade (visor). Locking gas filler door. Front fender stainless-steel gravel shields. Impala-style hood ornament. Tissue dispenser. San-Toy seat covers. Left-hand outside rearview mirror (standard in convertible). Right-hand outside rearview mirror. Radio antenna. License plate frame. Back-up lamp. Vacuumatic ashtray. Rubber heel protector. Underhood lamp. Luggage compartment lamp. Other standard factory and dealer-installed accessories. Powerglide, Deluxe only ($169).

HISTORICAL FOOTNOTES: Dealer introductions were held December 9, 1950. Model-year production totaled 1,250,803 units. Calendar-year sales were 1,118,096 cars. Chevrolet remained America's number one automaker.

No other economy-car dash board from the "Big Three" gave the buyer as much glitz as Chevrolet. To get this fancy an interior from the competition in 1951, a customer would have to buy a Mercury or a Chrysler for a lot more money.

CHAPTER 3

The rear fender trim on the 1952 Chevrolet Deluxe connected to the gravel guard, but they were separate on the 1951 Deluxe.

1952

Introduction
The 1952 Chevrolets were nearly identical to 1951 models. Chevrolet added five teeth to the 1952 grille. The hood badge was larger and had the Chevrolet name above the company's crest. The Deluxe rear fender gravel shield grew a little taller and incorporated a chrome spear running the length of the fender. The front parking light lenses were larger and the slots in the parking light housings disappeared. The dashboard remained the same as it had been in 1951, as did the tail lights.

The 1951 and 1952 Chevrolets can be a little hard to tell apart. The 1952 grille has teeth, and the parking light is larger and has no slotted bezel.

There were adjustments to the model lineup. The fastback Fleetline body made its last appearance in 1952 and was available only as a Deluxe two-door. The notchback Styleline Special had no chrome body strip. The similar Styleline Deluxe did have a chrome body strip, chrome gravel shields, and Deluxe lettering on the rear fender. The Styleline Deluxe line did not include a business coupe and added the Bel Air hardtop, the convertible, and the station wagon. This model adjustment eliminated three models and cut the total to 11.

Along with improved shock absorbers, Chevrolet catalogs touted selling features that included Fisher Unisteel body construction, Jumbo-Drum brakes with Dubl-Life linings, Center Point steering, Panoramic visibility, Safety-Sight instrument panel, Unitized Knee-Action front suspension, Finger-Tip gearshift and a ride stabilizer.

A new carburetor provided more positive acceleration and smoother performance. The splash-oiled 216 engine was in its last year in front of the standard Synchromesh manual transmission. The pressure-oiled 235 engine in the Powerglide cars recieved an automatic choke. The Styleline Special was offered in two- and four-door sedan models, a sport coupe (which wasn't a hardtop) and a business coupe.

I.D. NUMBERS: Serial numbers were stamped on a plate on the left front door hinge pillar. Engine numbers were stamped on the right side of the block near the fuel pump. The first symbol in the serial number indicated assembly plant as follows: (1) Flint, Michigan, (2) Tarrytown, New York, (3) St. Louis, Missouri., (5) Kansas City, Missouri., (6) Oakland, California, (8) Atlanta, Georgia, (9) Norwood, Ohio, (14) Baltimore, Maryland, (20) Los Angeles, California, (21) Janesville, Wisconsin. The second symbol indicated the model year: K=1952. The third symbol indicated the model and series: J=Special 1500 series, K=Deluxe 2100 series. The fourth symbol indicates the month of manufacture: A=January, etc. The last four symbols are the production sequence number in the specific factory. Serial numbers for Michigan-built 1952 Specials were: KJ-1001 to 19286. Engine numbers were: KA-1001 to 860773. Serial numbers for Michigan-built 1952 Deluxes were: KK-1001 to 115255. Deluxe engine numbers fit into same sequence listed for Special series above. The Fisher Body number plate on the right-hand side of the cowl gives additional information, such as the body style number (see second column in tables below), the body production sequence number, the trim (upholstery) number code and the paint number code.

PAINT COLORS : Monotone paint colors for 1952 were: No. 465 Onyx Black, No. 466 Birch Gray, No. 467 Dusk Gray, No. 469 Spring Green, No. 470 Emerald Green, No. 472 Admiral Blue, No. 477 Twilight Blue, No. 478 Sahara Beige, No. 479 Regal Maroon, No. 481 Cherry, No. 482 Honeydew, and No. 483 Saddle Brown. Two-tone color combinations for 1952 were: No. 468 Dusk Gray Metallic/Birch Gray, No. 471 Emerald Green Metallic/Spring Green, No. 473 Admiral Blue Metallic/Twilight Blue, No. 474 Spring Green/Emerald Green Metallic, No. 484 Birch Gray/Twilight Blue, No. 485 Birch Gray/Spring Green, No. 486 Sahara Beige/Saddle Brown Metallic, No. 487 Sahara Beige/Regal Maroon Metallic, No. 488 Saddle Brown Metallic/Sahara Beige, No. 489 Black/Birch Gray, No. 491 Black/Regal Maroon Metallic, No. 493 Black/Honeydew and No. 494 Birch Gray/Admiral Blue Poly.

Along with the automatic transmission, Powerglide-equipped Chevrolets came with more engine. Manual-transmission Chevrolets had the 216 cubic-inch, slash-oiled, babbit-bearing six from the 1930s, but with Powerglide, a Chevrolet came with the 235 cubic-inch six with pressurized oiling and insert bearings.

The Fleetline was nearly extinct in 1952 and was quickly being replaced by the Bel Air hardtop.

SPECIAL SERIES—SIX—1500 KJ: The Special series no longer included fastback Fleetline models. Specials had notchback styling, no chrome body molding, rubber gravel deflectors, black rubber windshield moldings, and open rear wheel housings. Nine exterior colors and four two-tone combinations were provided for all sedans, sport coupes and business coupes, including Styleline Specials. Two-tone gray interiors were featured, with seat upholstery of checkered pattern cloth, along with a three-spoke steering wheel with horn button.

SPECIAL SERIES 1500 KJ

STYLELINE SPECIAL SERIES					
Model No.	Body/Style No.	Body Type & Seating	Factory Price	Shipping Weight	Production Total
1503	1269	4d Sed-6P	$1,659	3,115 lbs.	35,460
1502	1211	2d Sed-6P	$1,603	3,085 lbs.	54,781
1524	1227	2d Spt Cpe-6P	$1,609	3,050 lbs.	8,906
1504	1227B	2d Bus Cpe-6P	$1,519	3,045 lbs.	10,359

DELUXE SERIES—SIX—2100 KK: Easily noticed distinctions between the Deluxe and the Special included body rub moldings on front fenders and doors, bright metal rear fender gravel guards with long chrome spears running the length of the fenders, rear fender skirts, Deluxe script logos directly above the gravel guards on the rear fender. Bright metal windshield moldings were featured as well. A two-spoke steering wheel carried a full horn ring. Deluxes also had ivory plastic control knobs with bright metal inserts, dome lamps with automatic door switches, two inside sun visors, richer interior trims and foam rubber cushions. Upholstery combinations were reversed, with a dark gray chevron-pattern cloth and lighter upper contrast panels. Station wagons, Bel Air hardtops and convertibles had their own exclusive trim. There were also four exterior paint colors for Bel Airs and 11 two-tone combinations, while convertibles came in 10 colors with five different top tones. Wagons offered four types of finish in combination with wood-grained trim panels.

The two-door Fleetline sedan was the sole fastback car in the Chevrolet line, and it came only with Deluxe trim. Powerglide was again only available in Deluxes and the Powerglide name was once again part of the trunk handle.

DELUXE SERIES 2100 KK

STYLELINE SUB-SERIES

Model No.	Body/Style No.	Body Type & Seating	Factory Price	Shipping Weight	Production Total
2103	1069	4d Sed-6P	$1,749	3,145 lbs.	319,736
2102	1011	2d Sed-6P	$1,696	3,110 lbs.	215,417
2124	1027	2d Spt Cpe-6P	$1,715	3,100 lbs.	36,954
2154	1037	2d Bel Air-6P	$1,992	3,215 lbs.	74,634
2134	1067	2d Conv-5P	$2,113	3,380 lbs.	11,975
2119	1062	4d Sta Wag-8P	$2,281	3,475 lbs.	12,756

FLEETLINE SUB-SERIES

2152	1007	2d Sed-6P	$1,696	3,110 lbs.	37,164

NOTE: Style number 1037 is a two-door pillarless hardtop coupe.

ENGINES:

ALL SERIES STANDARD SIX-CYL (MANUAL TRANSMISSION): Overhead-valve. Cast-iron block. Displacement: 216.5 cid. Bore and stroke: 3 ½ x 3 ¾ in. Compression ratio: 6.6:1. Brake hp: 92 at 3400 rpm. Four main bearings. Solid valve lifters. Carburetor: Rochester one-barrel B or BC (automatic choke on BC), or Stromberg BXOV-2 Model 380286, or Stromberg BXOV-25 Model 380270. Cooling system capacity: 15 qt. Crankcase capacity (less filter): 5 qt.

ALL SERIES STANDARD SIX-CYL (POWERGLIDE TRANSMISSION): Inline six. Overhead-valve. Cast-iron block. Displacement: 235.5 cid. Bore and stroke: 3 $^9/_{16}$ x 3 $^{15}/_{16}$ in. Four main bearings. Hydraulic valve lifters. Compression ratio: 6.7:1. Brake hp: 105 at 3600 rpm. Carburetor: Rochester one-barrel BC (Note: 3.55:1 gear ratio rear axle used with Powerglide transmission both years). Cooling system capacity: 15 qt. Crankcase capacity (less filter): 5 qt.

The 1952 Chevrolet Bel Air hardtop with Powerglide.

CHASSIS: Box girder frame. In convertible, a "VK" structure of I-beam members takes the place of engine rear support cross member. Knee-action front suspension with direct double-acting shock absorbers. Ride stabilizer. Rubber insulated semi-elliptic rear springs with metal covers. Direct double-acting hydraulic rear shock absorbers. Four-wheel hydraulic brakes with 11-in. drums. Wheelbase: (all) 115 in. Overall length: (passenger cars) 197.75 in., (station wagon) 198 ⅞ in. Front tread: (all) 57 in. Rear tread: (all) 58 ¾ in. Rear axle: Semi-floating with hypoid drive and 4.11:1 gear ratio. Torque tube drive with tubular propeller shaft, both fully enclosed. Tires: 6.70 x 15 blackwall on wide-base rims, 7.10 x 15 on convertible. Gas tank capacity: 16 gal. 6-volt electrical system.

OPTIONS: Directional signals. Dash panel ashtray (standard in Deluxe). Manual radio. Deluxe push-button radio. Under-dash heater and defroster. Deluxe in-dash heater and defroster. Full wheel discs. Wheel trim rings. Whitewall tires. Thirty-nine-hour stem wind clock (standard in Deluxe). Fender skirts (standard on Deluxe). No-Mar Fuel door guard. Door handle shields. Front and rear bumper wing tips. Master grille guard. Spotlight. Fog lamps. External sun shade (visor). Locking gas filler door. Front fender stainless steel gravel shields. Impala-style hood ornament. Tissue dispenser. San-Toy seat covers. Left-hand outside rearview mirror (standard in convertible). Right-hand outside rearview mirror. Radio antenna. License plate frame. Back-up lamp. Vacuumatic ashtray. Rubber heel protector. Under-hood lamp. Luggage compartment lamp. Other standard factory and dealer-installed accessories. Powerglide, Deluxe only ($178). E-Z-Eye glass. Ashtray (dash-type) now standard in both series. Availability of whitewalls was limited due to Korean War material restrictions.

HISTORICAL FOOTNOTES: Dealer introductions began Jan. 19, 1952. Model-year sales reached 827,317, despite Korean War manufacturing limitations. Calendar-year sales totaled 877,947 despite war. Whitewall tires were uncommon. An inferior chrome plating process was used this year. Chevrolet again ranked as the number one American automaker. In October 1952, the 1 millionth Powerglide-equipped Chevrolet was assembled, although the option was just 34 months old. The 28 millionth U.S. or Canadian Chevrolet car or truck was built in December 1952. The July 1952 issue of *Motor Trend* reported that General Motors was denying rumors that Chevrolet had a V-8 on the drawing board for the near future.

Now discover the <u>only</u> important difference between Chevrolet and high-priced cars . . .

The only important difference is in the cost . . . the money you save in buying and owning a Chevrolet! For Chevrolet brings you fine-car quality at today's lowest prices.

So see and drive a new Chevrolet and make these happy discoveries:

Find out that Chevrolet shares the distinction, quality and craftsmanship of Body by Fisher with some of America's most costly cars.

Find out that new Centerpoise Power makes Chevrolet surprisingly smooth in performance . . . surprisingly free of vibration and power impulses.

Find out that improvements in shock absorbers and steering make Chevrolet ride and handle in an altogether solid and satisfying big-car way.

See your Chevrolet dealer and discover that the *big* difference between Chevrolet and high-priced cars is the price itself . . . for Chevrolet is the lowest-priced line in its field! Why spend more when there's so little to gain by it? Chevrolet Division of General Motors, Detroit 2, Michigan.

Like the autumn woods, this De Luxe Sport Coupe has colorful beauty. Chevrolet offers 26 colors and two-tone combinations.

Takes to rough going like a field trial champion. Chevrolet's improved Knee-Action levels the bumps to make the roughest roads seem surprisingly smooth.

Safety a good hunter appreciates. Chevrolet's brakes are the largest in its field with full 11" brake drums and bonded linings that last up to twice as long.

Smooth as a bird in flight—that's Powerglide automatic transmission with extra-powerful valve-in-head engine. Optional on De Luxe models at extra cost.

Continuation of standard equipment and trim illustrated is dependent on availability of material.

MORE PEOPLE BUY CHEVROLETS THAN ANY OTHER CAR!

The Only Fine Cars **PRICED SO LOW!**

A *long drive* in this smart Sport Coupe leaves you rested, relaxed and ready for fun.

Pleasure? . . . Full measure!
Price? . . . Pleasant surprise!

If you think that high quality in a motor car goes hand in hand with high cost, your Chevrolet dealer has a very pleasant surprise for you.

You'll be surprised at the style and quality of Chevrolet's Body by Fisher . . . the *only* Body by Fisher in the low-price field.

You'll be surprised at the smoothness of new Centerpoise Power . . . with Chevrolet's famous valve-in-head engine centered, poised and cushioned in rubber by new high-side mountings.

You'll be surprised at the comfort of Chevrolet's improved Knee-Action ride . . . at the easy way this car handles and its solid feel on the road.

In *every* respect, this fine, big Chevrolet offers you a full measure of motoring pleasure. And yet—most pleasant surprise of all—it's the lowest-priced line in its field! See your Chevrolet dealer soon and satisfy yourself that there's no reason for paying more. Chevrolet Division of General Motors, Detroit 2, Michigan.

MORE PEOPLE BUY CHEVROLETS THAN ANY OTHER CAR!

The Only Fine Cars PRICED SO LOW!

Smooth as a fine tennis court—that's Powerglide automatic transmission with extra-powerful Valve-in-Head engine and Automatic Choke. Optional on De Luxe models at extra cost.

Colorful as the most scenic golf course. Chevrolet offers a choice of 26 solid colors and two-tone color combinations with color-matched interiors in De Luxe models.

Room for two foursomes in this handsome Chevrolet Station Wagon with all-steel Body by Fisher. Four doors for easier entrance and exit.

Continuation of standard equipment and trim illustrated is dependent on availability of material.

CHAPTER 4

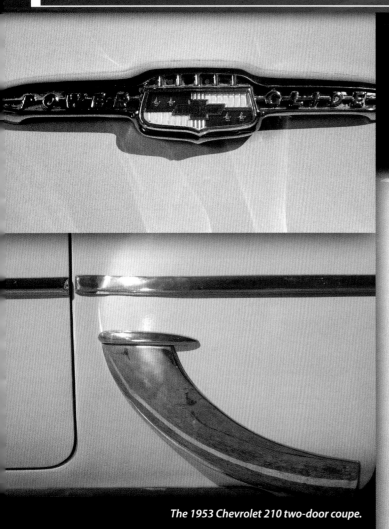

The 1953 Chevrolet 210 two-door coupe.

1953

Introduction

Few observers, or even those involved in its creation, could have imagined the long-lasting appeal of the little roadster Chevrolet unveiled in 1953. Only 300 Corvettes were built that year. They were cute little all-white cars with no back seat and carried Chevrolet's 235-cid six-cylinder engine.

The 1953 Chevrolet left the 1940s completely behind.

The car was based on the 1952 EX-122 show car and was one of the few Motorama dream cars to actually make it into real world production without major changes. Before eventually evolving into the all-American performance car icon it would later become, the Corvette was ticketed to be an affordable sports car for young adults. The fiberglass body was novel and practical, the car had great lines and seemed to ooze charisma. It was not long before Chevrolet brass began figuring out they were on to something big.

But the Corvette was not the only big news for Chevrolet in 1953. The other 1953 models received major styling changes and some new engineering. All new series designations broke ties to the past, and styling competed more squarely with Ford. All models featured a curved, one-piece windshield, shorter-looking, more abruptly rounded body styling, flatter hood, higher trunk lid, and a wider look from the rear. New styling details included a new chrome hood ornament, hood nameplate, new grille with three vertical fins on the center horizontal bar, extensions encircling the parking lamps, and new vertical tail/brake lights that also contained the backup lights. Large, round, chrome-dripping parking lights dominated the Chevrolet grille for 1953, making the car look like a little Cadillac.

The new model lineup came in four series. Chevrolet 150 models had no chrome body-side or window moldings, no fender skirts, and black rubber gravel shields. The 210 models had chrome body-side and window moldings and chrome gravel shields, but no fender skirts. Bel Air was now used as the name of a series with various body styles, rather than as the name of just the two-door hardtop. Bel Airs had a double molding treatment on the rear fenders with a contrasting color band containing the Bel Air nameplate and rear fender skirts. Chevrolet left the 1940s behind by dropping fastback styling completely for 1953, and the Fleetline name was no more. The Corvette, model 2934, was a series unto itself.

The Jet Age was fading, and the Space Age was coming.

Two new overhead-valve, inline six-cylinder engines (108 and 115 hp) provided improved performance and finally left the 1920s completely behind with the addition of insert bearings and fully pressurized oiling. Powerglide equaled the engines' good news by becoming a two-speed, self-shifting, fully automatic transmission that matched Ford's existing Ford-O-Matic and Chrysler Corporation's new Powerflite for '53. New Velvet-Pressure Jumbo-Drum brakes were easier to operate, and power steering was a new extra-cost option. New ignition-key starting brought the new engines to life.

Chevrolet was still number one in sales for 1953, but the competition was getting V-8s quickly, and competitors' styling was loudly telling Chevrolet that the Bowtie could not rest on its laurels for long.

I.D. NUMBERS: Serial numbers were stamped on a plate on the left front door hinge pillar. The first symbol in the serial number indicated the model and series: A=One-Fifty 1500 series, B=Two-Ten 2100 series, C=Bel Air 2400 series. E=Corvette 2900 series. The second and third symbols indicated the model year: 53=1953. The fourth symbol indicates the assembly plant as follows: (A) Atlanta, Georgia, (B) Baltimore, Maryland, (F) Flint, Michigan, (J) Janesville, Wisconsin, (K) Kansas City, Missouri, (L) Los Angeles, California, (O) Oakland, California, (S) St. Louis, Missouri, (T) Tarrytown, New York and (N) Norwood, Ohio. The last six symbols are the production sequence number in the specific factory. (Special 1500) Serial numbers A53( )-001001 to A53( )-228961, (Deluxe 2100) Serial numbers B53( )-001001 to 228961, (Bel Air) Serial numbers C53( )-001001 to 228961. Corvettes for 1953 were numbered E53F001001 to E53F001300. Engine numbers were stamped on the right side of the block near the fuel pump. Engine numbers (all models): LA-1001 to 1183450. Engine numbers consisted of four to seven numbers with a prefix or suffix. The prefix or suffix indicated year, engine size, factory, type of valve lifter and other peculiarities. Restorers can consult Chevrolet shop manuals or master parts catalogs for this type of information. The Fisher Body number plate on the right-hand side of the cowl gives additional information, such as the body style number (see second column in tables below), the body production sequence number, the trim (upholstery) number code and the paint number code. Since the Corvette bodies were virtually handmade, they did not carry standard Fisher Body Style Numbers as did other GM cars. The Corvette model number consisted of the four digits 2934, which also served as the body style number for the early production years.

PAINT COLORS: Monotone paint colors for 1953 were: No. 480 Onyx Black, No. 490 Driftwood Gray, No. 496 Dusk Gray, No. 498 Surf Green, No. 499 Woodland Green, No. 501 Regatta Blue, No. 503 Horizon Blue, No. 504 Sahara Beige, No. 505 Madeira Maroon, No. 506 Target Red, No. 507 Campus Cream, No. 508 Sun Gold and No. 509 Saddle Brown. Two-tone color combinations for 1953 were: No. 497 Dusk Gray/Driftwood Gray, No. 500 Woodland Green/Surf Green, No. 502 Regatta Blue/Horizon Blue, No. 510 India Ivory/Horizon Blue, No. 511 India Ivory/Regatta Blue, No. 512 Campus Green/Woodland Green, No. 513 Woodland Green/Campus Green, No. 514 Saddle Brown/Shara Beige, No. 515 Sahara Beige/Saddle Brown, No. 516 India Ivory/Sungold and No. 517 Target Red/India Ivory.

SPECIAL 150 SERIES—SIX-CYL—1500 A: Cars with former Special-level features and trim were renamed One-Fifty or 150 models. The designation came from the first three digits of the numerical series code. The sport coupe became the club coupe, and the 150 station wagon was called the Handyman. Easy identifiers included rubber windshield molding, plain body sides without moldings, rubber gravel guards, no rocker panel molding, unskirted rear wheel housings, and no series nameplate. On the inside of Special 150s there was a standard steering wheel, single sun visor, and plain upholstery. The One-Fifty station wagon had safety sheet side door windows in place of safety plate glass and was rated a six-passenger car.

SPECIAL 150 SERIES

Model No.	Body/Style No.	Body Type & Seating	Factory Price	Shipping Weight	Production Total
1503	1269	4d Sed-6P	$1,670	3,215 lbs.	54,207
1502	1211	2d Sed-6P	$1,613	3,180 lbs.	79,416
1524	1227	2d Clb Cpe-6P	$1,620	3,140 lbs.	6,993
1504	1227B	2d Bus Cpe-3P	$1,524	3,140 lbs.	13,555
1509	1262F	4d Sta Wag-6P	$2,010	3,420 lbs.	22,408

NOTE: *Style Number 1227B has a single seat (front), fixed rear quarter windows and rear storage space with raised floor. Style number 1262F has two seats (folding second seat) and Plexiglas "Safety Seal" side windows.*

DELUXE 210 SERIES—SIX-CYL—2100 B: Cars with the former Deluxe-level features and trim were now called Two-Ten or 210 models. This new designation also took its name from the first three digits of a numerical series code. The sport coupe became the club coupe. The pillarless hardtop was not a Bel Air. The six-passenger station wagon with folding second seat was called the Handyman, as was the same version with Special trim. The eight-passenger station wagon was called the Townsman. The Townsman had three seats with the second and third units being stationary but completely removable. The 210 convertible was deleted in midyear and the 210 Townsman station wagon was also dropped for 1954, along with the 210 sport coupe. External identification of 210s was afforded by horizontal lower belt moldings running from front to rear, chrome windshield and window moldings, rocker panel moldings and bright metal rear gravel guards with short spears at the top. A two-spoke steering wheel with horn ring was used. Standard equipment also included cigarette lighter, dash panel ashtray, dual sun visors and 39-hour stem-wind clock. Heaters and radios were optional. Interior door handles used on 210 models had bright metal inserts in the black plastic knobs. Other interior appointments included foam rubber seat cushion pads in front seats and in rear seats of sedans and coupes, front armrests in all models, rear armrests in sedans and coupes, rear compartment ashtray in four-door sedans, one ashtray in each armrest of two-door sedans and coupes, and bright metal moldings on rear quarter panels of sedans and coupes.

DELUXE 210 SERIES

Model No.	Body/Style No.	Body Type & Seating	Factory Price	Shipping Weight	Production Total
2103	1069W	4d Sed-6P	$1,761	3,250 lbs.	332,497
2102	1011W	2d Sed-6P	$1,707	3,215 lbs.	247,455
2124	1027	2d Clb Cpe-6P	$1,726	3,190 lbs.	23,961
2154	1037	2d Spt Cpe-6P	$1,967	3,295 lbs.	14,045
2134	1067	2d Conv-5P	$2,093	3,435 lbs.	5,617
2109	1062F	4d Sta Wag-6P	$2,123	3,450 lbs.	18,258
2119	1062	4d Sta Wag-8P	$2,273	3,495 lbs.	7,988

NOTE: *Two-Ten body/style numbers are similar to Bel Air body/style numbers, except for suffixes. Style Number 1011W, 1037 and 1067 have lowering rear quarter windows. The style number 1062F 210 Townsman station wagon varies from the "150" Townsman in that safety plate-glass door windows are used.*

The 1953 Chevrolet grille usually came with only three teeth, but some Chevrolet collectors claim dealerships could install extra teeth as accessories.. This Bel Air had the extra teeth and a full compliment of grille and bumper guards. The large, round parking lights make the 1953 Chevrolet look like a baby '53 Cadillac.

BEL AIR—SIX-CYL—SERIES 2400 C: The Bel Air added a double molding on the rear fender pontoon. It enclosed a panel that was decorated with a short, wide-ribbed beauty molding, Bel Air script and Chevrolet crest on the leading edge above a chrome gravel shield. All 210 trim features and equipment were incorporated, plus rear fender skirts, double windshield pillar moldings, extra wide window reveals on sedans and saddle moldings on sport coupes and convertibles. Exposed bright metal roof bows and dashboard-mounted rearview mirrors were standard in Bel Air sport coupes. Upholstery materials were a few notches up the luxury scale.

BEL AIR SERIES

Model No.	Body/Style No.	Body Type & Seating	Factory Price	Shipping Weight	Production Total
2403	1069WD	4d Sed-6P	$1,874	3,275 lbs.	246,284
2402	1011WD	2d Sed-6P	$1,620	3,230 lbs.	144,401
2454	1037D	2d Spt Cpe-6P	$2,051	3,310 lbs.	99,047
2434	1067D	2d Conv-5P	$2,175	3,470 lbs.	24,047

CORVETTE—SIX-CYL—SERIES 2934 E: The new 1953 Corvette had a fiberglass body, chrome-framed grille with 13 heavy vertical chrome bars, rounded front fenders with recessed headlights with wire screen covers, no side windows or outside door handles, a wraparound windshield and protruding, fender-integrated tail lights. The interior featured a floor-mounted shifter for the Powerglide two-speed automatic transmission and oil pressure, battery, water temperature and fuel gauges, plus a tachometer and clock. Each 1953 Corvette was virtually hand-built and a lot of minor changes were made during the production run. All of the first-year cars were Polo White with Sportsman Red interiors. All had black canvas convertible tops that manually folded into a storage space behind the seats. Other 1953-only features included special valve covers, a one-piece carburetor linkage and a small trunk mat. Short exhaust extensions were used on all '53s (and early '54s) because they were prone to drawing exhaust fumes into the car through the vent windows. A black oilcloth window storage bag was provided to protect the 1953 Corvette's removable plastic side windows when stowed in the trunk.

CORVETTE SERIES 2934 E

Model No.	Body/Style No.	Body Type & Seating	Factory Price	Shipping Weight	Production Total
2934	2934	2-dr Rds-2P	$3,498	2,705 lbs.	300

ENGINES:

ALL SERIES STANDARD SIX-CYL (MANUAL TRANSMISSION): Overhead-valve. Cast-iron block. Displacement: 235.5 cid. Bore and stroke: 3 $^9/_{16}$ x 3 $^{15}/_{16}$. Compression ratio: 7.1:1. Brake hp: 108 at 3600 rpm. Four main bearings. Solid valve lifters. Carburetor: Rochester one-barrel B-type Model 7007161 or Carter one-barrel Model 2101S. Cooling system capacity without heater: 15 qt. Crankcase capacity (less filter): 5 qt.

The toothy, sexy 1953 Corvette roadster. (Nicky Wright)

ALL SERIES STANDARD SIX-CYL (POWERGLIDE TRANSMISSION): Overhead-valve. Cast-iron block. Displacement: 235.5 cid. Bore and stroke: 3 $^9/_{16}$ x 3 $^{15}/_{16}$ in. Compression ratio: 7.5:1. Brake hp: 115 at 3600 rpm. Four main bearings. Hydraulic valve lifters. Carburetor: Rochester BC type one-barrel Model 7007200 or Carter one-barrel Model 2101S. (A transmission oil cooler and 3.55:1 axle ratio were used with Powerglide.) Cooling system capacity without heater: 15 qt. Crankcase capacity (less filter): 5 qt.

CHASSIS: Wheelbase: (all series except Corvette) 115 in. Overall length: (all passenger cars) 195 ½ in., (all station wagons) 197 $^7/_6$ in. Front tread: (all) 56.69 in. Rear tread: (all) 58.75 in. Tires: (convertible with Powerglide) 7.10 x 15 four-ply, (Townsman station wagon) 6.70 x 15 six-ply, (all others) 6.70 x 15 four-ply. Standard rear axle ratio: 3.7:1. Fuel capacity: 16 gal. 6-volt electrical system. Corvette: Wheelbase: 102 inches. Overall length: 167 inches. Front tread: 57 inches. Rear tread: 58.8 inches. Steel disk wheels. Tires: 6.70 x 15. Front suspension: Coil springs, tubular shock absorbers and stabilizer bar. Rear suspension: Leaf springs, tube shocks and solid rear axle. Drum brakes. Axle ratio: 3.55:1.

OPTIONS: Power steering ($178). Custom radio push-button. Custom Deluxe radio. Recirculating heater and defroster (under dash type). Air Flow heater and defroster (dashboard type). E-Z-Eye tinted glass. Autronic Eye automatic headlamp dimmer. White sidewall tires. Directional signals. Back-up lights. Bumper guards (second pair, front or rear). Front fender gravel shields. Door handle shields. Windshield sun shade (visor). Full wheel discs. Accessory "bird-type" hood ornament. Fender skirts on 150 models. License plate frame. Front and rear bumper tip guards. Stem-wind clock on 150 models. Radio antenna. Locking gas filler door. Venti-pane wind deflectors. Left-hand outside rearview mirror. Fog lights. Traffic light viewer. Tissue dispenser. Vacuumatic ashtray. Non-glare rearview mirror. No-Mar fuel door trim. Under-hood light. San-Toy seat covers. Powerglide ($178). Other standard factory and dealer-installed accessories.

HISTORICAL FOOTNOTES: Dealer introductions occurred in January 1953. Model-year sales totaled 1,356,413. Calendar-year sales reached 1,477,287. A completely new body was offered with wraparound backlight on all models except the club coupe, convertible and station wagon. Powerglide models now had full-pressure lubrication. Powerglide was available in 210 and Bel Air lines only. Seventeen models were the most ever offered by Chevrolet. It was also the first year for Chevrolet power steering. Chevrolet remained America's number one automaker.

All '53 Corvettes came with whitewalls and two-spinner hubcaps. (Nicky Wright)

Note the factory mesh headlight covers on this 1953 Corvette. (Nicky Wright)

The Corvette carried the 235.5-cid inline six. (Jerry Heasley)

A two-spoke steering wheel was part of a simple Corvette interior.

(Jerry Heasley)

Edward Blanck Sr. poses with a new 1953 Chevrolet Bel Air sedan. Blanck Chevrolet opened for business in 1928 in Brownsburg, Indiana, and his descendants still run the business in the 21st century. Blanck had reasons to be happy. In 1953, all Chevrolet engines finally got full pressurized oiling and insert bearings, and Powerglide became a fully automatic transmission. (Blanck family collection)

Technically, the 1950s began in 1950, but when did the 1950s begin in a cultural sense?

Some point out that what Americans think of as the 1930s culture really stretched up through 1941 when the war disrupted everything. The postwar, baby-booming 1940s really lasted through about 1953. What Americans think of as the 1950s, with rock music, drive-ins, cruising culture, sock hops, and leather jackets began with *Blackboard Jungle* in 1954, lasted through about 1964, and were immortalized by *American Graffiti* and *Happy Days* in retrospect. The dreaded '60s, with war protests, hippies, psychedelia, and the Beatles, faded in around 1965 and lasted to about 1973 when the '70s

finally reared its yellow, polyester happy-face with the gas crunch and disco beats of 1974.

It's arguable that Chevrolet was still living in the 1940s until the last fastback Fleetline rolled off the assembly line in 1952. The lightly colored, airy hardtops had already forecast the optimistic future through the early-'50s, and in 1953, Chevrolet was completely into the 1950s. Even the four-door sedans had nothing to remind people of the 1940s. The interiors came in various colors, and the windshields were one piece. The Bel Air hardtop windshield was lower and flatter across its top border, which gave the '53 Bel Air a much wider, lower appearance inside and out. The rear of the cars had a high, flat look, and the tail lights were no longer small and way down low, but rather, they were large and high.

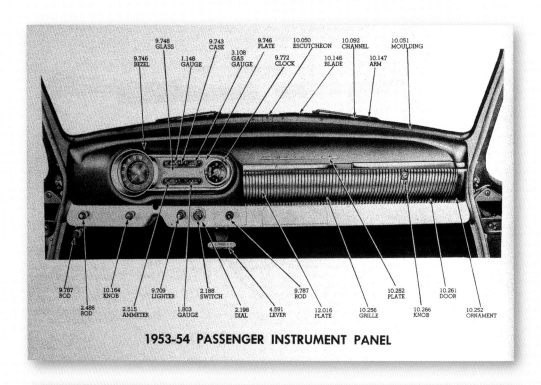

1953-54 PASSENGER INSTRUMENT PANEL

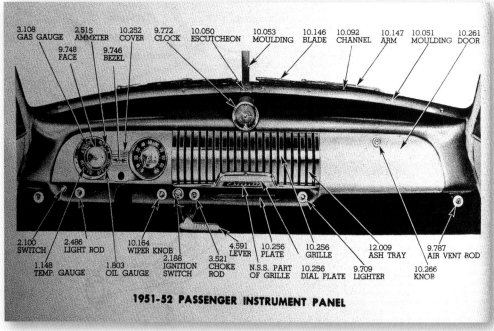

1951-52 PASSENGER INSTRUMENT PANEL

Direct comparison of the 1951-'52 Chevrolet dash (bottom) and the 1953-'54 Chevrolet dash (top).

The cars didn't even drive like traditional Chevrolets anymore. Even the entry-level 150 model with a manual-transmission had a highway-speed rear axle ratio and optional power steering. The best news of all was that all Chevrolet engines finally had insert bearings and fully pressurized oiling, which brought the Chevrolet drive train clear out of the 1930s. The Powerglide joined the 1950s by becoming a self-shifting, fully automatic transmission, and it no longer had anything in common with the non-shifting, single-speed Buick Dynaflow. A '53 Chevrolet with Powerglide was the snappiest, quickest accelerating, most modern-feeling car the company had ever made.

The front of the 1953 Chevrolet had giant, round parking lights at each end of the grille, and the little Chevy looked like a baby Cadillac. The higher oval tail lights looked like part of the car and made Pontiac's low, round tail lights look old-fashioned—like they didn't belong on a 1950s car. Chevrolet model names reflected the times, too. The Special and Deluxe names that dated to the 1930s were gone and replaced with 150 and 210—modern, scientific-sounding, numerical names that brought to mind high technology instead of Art Deco beauty.

The 1954 Chevrolet smiled even wider with more teeth, and the parking lights became oval and moved the ends of the grille, where they became part of the car instead of attention-getting ornaments. Chevrolet enthusiasts point out that, while the 1953 and '54 Chevrolets look a lot alike, they don't share body parts from the windshield forward, and parts cars have to be an exact match to help the restorer.

The 1953 and '54 Chevrolets did well in sales, and they were Chevrolet's great leap out of the '40s and into the '50s, but they had a short life. Changing times and changing Chevrolets would make them instantly old-fashioned, and they were forgotten for many years until rediscovered decades later and given much-deserved recognition.

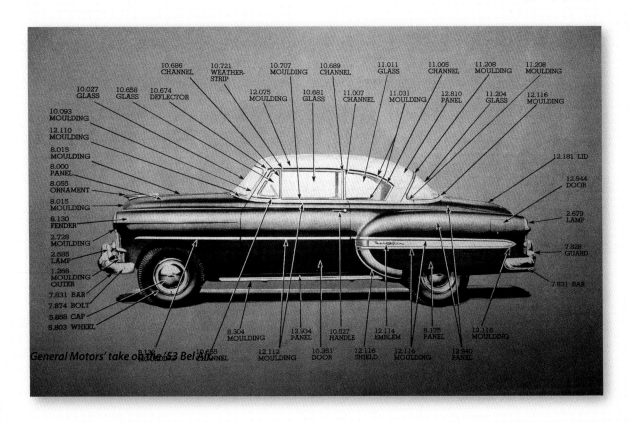

General Motors' take on the '53 Bel Air.

Chevrolet's striking Bel Air Sport Coupe. With 3 great new series, Chevrolet offers the widest choice of models in its field.

How Chevrolet's new high-compression horsepower takes you more places on less gas . . .

You see *two* pretty exciting kinds of horsepower in our picture up there.

One is the rarin', buckin', four-legged kind of horsepower that makes a rodeo a popular place to go.

The other kind is the smooth, quiet horsepower of that fine, spankin' new Chevrolet.

The beauty of Chevrolet's new power is this: It gives you faster acceleration and passing ability. More "steam" for steep hills. And all on a lot less gas—and on *regular* gas at that!

How can you get more power on less gas? High compression is the answer. The fuel mixture is squeezed much tighter so that the engine wrings much more power out of it.

Chevrolet brings you the benefits of high-compression power whether you choose the mighty 115-h.p. "Blue-Flame" engine teamed with Powerglide* or the 108-h.p. "Thrift-King" engine with standard transmission.

But high-compression power is only one of the things you'll like about the new Chevrolet. You'll like the extra-low upkeep; the smoother, softer ride; the easier braking action. And there's much more, including Power Steering,* if you wish, to do eighty per cent of the work of turning the wheel!

Your Chevrolet dealer will gladly demonstrate whenever you drop in. Chevrolet Division of General Motors, Detroit 2, Michigan.

Optional at extra cost. Combination of Powerglide automatic transmission and 115-h.p. "Blue-Flame" engine available on "Two-Ten" and Bel Air models only. Power Steering available on all models.

MORE PEOPLE BUY CHEVROLETS THAN ANY OTHER CAR!

NEW *Chevrolet for* 1953

THE BEL AIR 2-DOOR SEDAN

Startlingly Underline New!
Wonderfully Different!

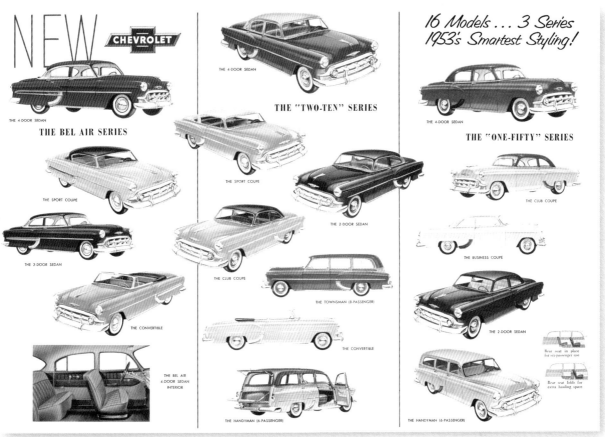

NEW CHEVROLET

THE 4-DOOR SEDAN

THE BEL AIR SERIES

THE SPORT COUPE

THE 2-DOOR SEDAN

THE CONVERTIBLE

THE BEL AIR 4-DOOR SEDAN INTERIOR

THE 4-DOOR SEDAN

THE "TWO-TEN" SERIES

THE SPORT COUPE

THE CLUB COUPE

THE TOWNSMAN (8-PASSENGER)

THE CONVERTIBLE

THE HANDYMAN (6-PASSENGER)

THE 2 DOOR SEDAN

16 Models . . . 3 Series
1953's Smartest Styling!

THE 4-DOOR SEDAN

THE "ONE-FIFTY" SERIES

THE CLUB COUPE

THE BUSINESS COUPE

THE 2-DOOR SEDAN

Rear seat in place for six-passenger use

Rear seat folds for extra hauling space

THE HANDYMAN (6-PASSENGER)

CHAPTER 5

Chevrolet's most popular model in 1954—the
Bel Air four-door sedan. Bel Air interiors were
color-coordinated with the exterior.

1954

Introduction

This was the last year that a Chevrolet had a prewar bulge for a rear fender—the last vestige of the prewar world when fenders were bolted onto cars as separate pieces. Chevrolet looked back to the past for the last time in 1954, and this bulge was destined to disappear completely in 1955 as it already had from Oldsmobile, Buick and Cadillac.

The parking lights for the 1954 Chevrolet were no longer fancy ornaments as they had been in 1953. The parking lights were smoothly integrated parts of the entire grille.

The 1954 Chevrolet didn't change much in silhouette, but it was as big a step toward more modern styling as 1953 had been from 1952. The round, dominant, Cadillac-ish parking lights from 1953 disappeared, and Chevrolet replaced them with unobtrusive oval parking lights on the extreme ends of the grill that went unnoticed until they started flashing for a turn. The parking lights were part of the car instead of expressive, Art-Deco add-ons. The tail lights were taller, longer, more vertical, and slightly hooded at the top. The grille smiled wider with more teeth—a younger, more enthusiastic smile than the more grandmotherly 1953 models. The ends of the front bumper bulged and reached ahead of the car.

Engine horsepower on manual-transmission Chevrolets had been elevated to 115, and the engines in front of the Powerglide reached new heights with 125 hp. All the Chevrolet engines had full-pressure oiling and insert bearings, and Powerglide cars had hydraulic valve lifters. Rear axle ratios were 3.70 for manual-shift cars and 3.55 for Powerglide cars, making for good highway cruising speeds for even base-model Chevrolets.

The 1954 Chevrolet was the boldest, most forward-looking Chevrolet to date, and while collector enthusiasm for the 1955 V-8 Chevrolets tends to overshadow the 1954, the '54s have a collector fan base all their own. Some collectors like cars that are tied to a more distant past, and 1954 was the last year a Chevrolet had a predominantly prewar drive train. This trait causes some collectors to ignore them as old-fashioned, while other enthusiasts love them for their nostalgic ties to the past.

I.D. NUMBERS: Serial numbers were stamped on a plate on the left front door hinge pillar. The first symbol in the serial number indicated the model and series: A=One-Fifty 1500 series, B=Two-Ten 2100 series, C=Bel Air 2400 series. E-Corvette 2934 series. The second and third symbols indicated the model year: 54=1954. The fourth symbol indicates the assembly plant as follows: (A) Atlanta, Georgia, (B) Baltimore, Maryland, (F) Flint, Michigan, (J) Janesville, Wisconsin, (K) Kansas City, Missouri, (L) Los Angeles, California, (N) Norwood, Ohio, (O) Oakland, California, (S) St. Louis, Missouri, and (T) Tarrytown, New York. The last six symbols are the production sequence number in the specific factory. Special 1500 Serial numbers A54( )-001001 to A54-174684, Deluxe 2100 Serial numbers B54( )-001001 to 174684, Bel Air Serial numbers C54( )-001001 to 174684. Corvette 2934 Serial numbers E54S001001 to E54S004640. Engine numbers were stamped on the right side of the block near the fuel pump. Engine numbers: (all models) 01001Z54 to 1024930. The engine numbers for 1954 models used the suffix YG. Engine numbers consisted of four to seven numbers with a prefix or suffix. The prefix or suffix indicated year, engine size, factory, type of valve lifter and other peculiarities. Restorers can consult Chevrolet shop manuals or master parts catalogs for this type of information. The Fisher Body number plate on the right-hand side of the cowl gives additional information, such as the body style number (see second column in tables below), the body production sequence number, the trim (upholstery) number code and the paint number code. Since the Corvette bodies were virtually handmade, they did not carry standard Fisher Body Style Numbers as did other GM cars.

PAINT COLORS: Monotone paint colors for 1954 were: No. 540 Onyx Black, No. 541Surf Green, No. 542 Bermuda Green, No. 543 Horizon Blue, No. 544 Biscayne Blue, No. 545 Shoreline Beige, No. 546 Saddle Brown, No. 547 India Ivory, No. 548 Shadow Gray, No. 549 Morocco Red, No. 550 Romany Red, No. 551 Fiesta Cream, No. 552 Turquoise, and No. 553 Pueblo Tan. Two-tone color combinations for 1954 were: No. 556 Shoreline Beige/Bermuda Green, No. 555 India Ivory/Surf Green, No. 556 India Ivory/Horizon Blue, No. 557 India Ivory/Biscayne Blue, No. 558 Bermuda Green/Shoreline Beige, No. 559 Shoreline Beige/Saddle Brown, No. 560 India Ivory/Onyx Black, No. 561 India Ivory/Romany Red, No. 562 Bermuda Green/Fiesta Cream, No. 563 India Ivory/Turquoise, No. 564 Shoreline Beige/Pueblo Tan, N0. 565 Morocco Red/Shoreline Beige, and No. 566 Shoreline Beige/Morocco Red.

The magnificent 1954 Chevrolet Bel Air station wagon was a special order that only saw 8,156 buyers. The Corvette was the only Chevrolet more expensive than the Bel Air wagon in 1954. Chevrolet would not field such a fancy wagon again until the 1966 Caprice.

SPECIAL 150 SERIES—SIX-CYL—1500 A: These continued to be General Motors' least-expensive cars. The 150s sedans and wagons lacked all side trim on the bodies and rockers as they had in 1953 and had the same utilitarian black rubber moldings around the windows and on the rear fender gravel guards. The tail lights included the white lenses for the back-up lights, but they had to be wired up by the dealers as optional equipment on the 150s. Chevrolet said the 150 interiors were "smartly fashioned of durable materials" like black window knobs and very plain upholstery.

Making Powerglide available even on 150s was one step toward modernizing even the most base-model Chevrolet.

The club coupe was gone and the business coupe was renamed the "utility sedan." This model had no back seat, but had a raised rear compartment floor instead.

SPECIAL 150 SERIES

Model No.	Body/Style No.	Body Type & Seating	Factory Price	Shipping Weight	Production Total
1503	1269W	4d Sed-6P	$1,680	3,210 lbs.	32,430
1502	1211W	2d Sed-6P	$1,623	3,165 lbs.	64,855
1509	1262F	4d Sta Wag-6P	$2,020	3,455 lbs.	21,404
1512	1211WB	2d Utl Sed-3P	$1,539	3,145 lbs.	10,770

DELUXE 210 SERIES—SIX-CYL—2100 B: Identifying a 210 for 1954 was about the same as it had been in 1953. There was a big jump in trim and appointments when a buyer set down the cash for a 210 over a 150. They got chrome body side moldings, chrome windshield moldings, chrome window moldings, rocker panel moldings, bright metal gravel guards, genuine carpets in the rear compartment and durable cloth seats with vinyl contrasting panels in four different color schemes. The 210 club coupe was sometimes called the Del Ray and came with all-vinyl, waffle pattern upholstery and matching two-tone door panels. The 210 Handyman station wagon was upholstered with long-wearing vinyl materials of contrasting colors and textures, including horizontally ribbed door panel inserts. The 210 convertible and Townsman station wagon were dropped.

DELUXE 210 SERIES

Model No.	Body/Style No.	Body Type & Seating	Factory Price	Shipping Weight	Production Total
2103	1069W	4d Sed-6P	$1,771	3,230 lbs.	235,146
2102	1011W	2d Sed-6P	$1,717	3,185 lbs.	194,498
2124	1011WA	2d Del Ray Cpe-6P	$1,782	3,185 lbs.	66,403
2109	1062F	4d Sta Wag-6P	$2,133	3,470 lbs.	27,175

NOTE: *Style number 1062F was the Handyman station wagon with two seats. The rear seat was most often a folding type.*

The Chevrolet six was its most high-tech to-date in 1954. On the Powerglide models, the six had a higher-lift camshaft and hydraulic valve lifters, and horsepower reached 125.

BEL AIR—SIX-CYL—SERIES 2400 C: The Bel Air series strode into 1954 with the same assortment of extra equipment and features as 1953—full genuine carpeting, newly designed full wheel discs, horizontally ebbed vinyl door panels, and an electric clock. The sport coupe had special Fashion Fiesta two-tone upholstery, rear pillar courtesy lights, chrome-plated inside roof garnish moldings and bright metal exposed roof bows. The convertible interior seemed even richer, with two-tone all-vinyl trims and snap-on boot cover. The rearview mirror was no longer mounted atop the dashboard on hardtops and convertibles. The full-length chrome spear with double-moldings on rear fenders enclosed a color-sweep, the Bel Air name, and a Chevrolet crest. Bright-metal double windshield pillar moldings and window moldings, bright belt-line molding, rocker panel moldings, bright metal gravel guards, and rear wheel fender skirts made the Bel Air a handsome package for the economy-class money.

The Bel Air station wagon was extra-special and the most expensive Chevrolet ever offered besides the Corvette. The Bel Air wagon came with striking, high-quality imitation wood trim beginning at the top of the front doors and widening slightly as it swept to the rear of the car above the rear fender, and the interior was color-keyed to the exterior color. The Bel Air was a full eight-passenger wagon with a metal trimmed step into the right-rear door to allow access to the third seat. The second seat had a swanky chrome handlebar on the right side. The two rear seats were moveable, making the Bel Air wagon as useful as its less fancy sisters. Chevrolet would not produce such a luxurious, highly trimmed station wagon again until the Caprice wagon in 1966.

BEL AIR SERIES

Model No.	Body/Style No.	Body Type & Seating	Factory Price	Shipping Weight	Production Total
2403	1069WD	4d Sed-6P	$1,684	3,255 lbs.	248,750
2402	1011WD	2d Sed-6P	$1,830	3,220 lbs.	143,573
2454	1037D	2d Spt Cpe-6P	$2,061	3,300 lbs.	66,378
2434	1067D	2d Conv-5P	$2,165	3,445 lbs.	19,383
2419	1062D	4d Sta Wag-8P	$2,263	3,540 lbs.	8,156

NOTE: *Style number 1062D was the Bel Air station wagon.*

CORVETTE—SIX-CYL—SERIES E2934: For all practical purposes the 1953 and 1954 Corvettes were the same. Minor changes were made to the window storage bag, air cleaners, starter and locations of the fuel and brake lines. Unlike the previous year's model, 1954s were available in Pennant Blue, Sportsman Red and Black, in addition to Polo White. The soft top was now offered in beige. A new style of valve cover was used. It was held on by four bolts through the outside lip instead of two center studs. The valve cover decals were different with larger lettering. The optional radio had Conelrad National Defense System icons on its face. In early 1954, the original two-handled hood latch was changed to a single-handle design. Six-cylinder Corvettes after serial number E54S003906 had integrated dual-port air cleaners. A clip to hold the ventipanes closed was added in late 1954 and also used on all 1955 models.

CORVETTE SERIES

Model No.	Body/Style No.	Body Type & Seating	Factory Price	Shipping Weight	Production Total
2934	2934	2-dr Rds-2P	$2,774	2,705 lbs.	3,640

The Bel Air wagon appeared at the end of the true "woodie" era, but well before the fake-wood era of the late-1960s, and its imitation wood trim was some of the most tasteful ever applied to an American car.

A sleek and sweeping beauty—
and an ideal family car. There's
room for six with room to
spare in the beautiful Body by
Fisher. Interiors are smartly
appointed and color-keyed to the
exterior finish of your choice.

△ The "Two-Ten" 4-Door Sedan
The "One-Fifty" 4-Door Sedan ▽

Beautiful Chevrolet styling and
solid Chevrolet value are yours
in this thrifty "One-Fifty"
model. You'll be surprised and
delighted at the many fine-car
features offered in Chevrolet's
lowest priced four-door sedan.

5

The "One-Fifty" Utility Sedan

Here's another brand-new Chevrolet model for 1954!
Extra load space is the outstanding advantage
offered by the smart, thrifty "One-Fifty" Utility Sedan.
The entire rear compartment of this three-passenger
model is devoted to cargo space. The perfect
answer for salesmen, businessmen, farmers—in fact,
for anyone who needs a dual-purpose car.
The raised rear floor makes loading and
unloading easy.

11

The new 1954 Chevrolet Bel Air 4-Door Sedan. With three great series, Chevrolet offers the most beautiful choice of models in its field.

Some sensible reasons why it's more <u>fun</u> to own a Chevrolet...

Maybe we can't all be quite as lucky as the man in our picture. Not everyone has a blue-jeaned daughter with a touch of tomboy in her to take fishin'.

But you can easily share his pleasure in going places in that new Chevrolet. It's engineered to be just plain *fun* to own, from the day you drive it home until the day you trade it in.

IT PUTS THE PLEASURE BACK IN DRIVING. Here's one car that's *easy* to handle in today's traffic. You really get a kick out of its quick, quiet response to your foot on the accelerator (highest compression power of any leading low-priced car). You feel good about the smooth, easy way it stops on a dime (biggest brakes in the low-price field). You sense with relaxing pleasure that you've got a lot of car under you (only car in its field with the extra strength of Fisher Unisteel

Construction and a full length box-girder frame).

IT'S FUN TO BE THRIFTY in a new Chevrolet. And you *are* thrifty. For this fine, big Chevrolet is priced below all other lines of cars. And Chevrolet's great name for economy of operation and upkeep is growing even greater this year. That new high-compression power means not only more fun per gallon, but important gasoline savings as well!

SURE AS SEA WATER'S SALTY, your Chevrolet dealer has just the right model to make a gay and care-free companion for *your* family fun. Let him show you how Chevrolet, as the world's largest builder of automobiles, can give you more car for your money. And while you're there, be sure you *drive* this new Chevrolet —if only for the fun of it. . . . Chevrolet Division of General Motors, Detroit 2, Michigan.

NOW AUTOMATIC WINDOW AND SEAT CONTROLS. This year's Chevrolet offers you any or all of the latest automatic power features and controls. If you like, you can have the extra-cost options of Automatic Front Window and Seat Controls on Bel Air and "Two-Ten" models, and Power Brakes on Powerglide models, as well as Power Steering and zippy, thrifty Powerglide on all models.

MORE PEOPLE BUY CHEVROLETS THAN ANY OTHER CAR!

ENGINES:

ALL SERIES STANDARD SIX-CYL (MANUAL TRANSMISSION): Overhead-valve. Cast-iron block. Displacement: 235.5 cid. Bore and stroke: 3 $^9/_{16}$ x 3 $^{15}/_{16}$. Compression ratio: 7.5:1. Brake hp: 115 at 3700 rpm. Four main bearings. Solid valve lifters. Carburetor: Rochester one-barrel "B"-type Model 7007181 or Carter one-barrel 2102S. Cooling system capacity without heater: 16 qt. Crankcase capacity (less filter): 5 qt.

ALL SERIES STANDARD SIX-CYL (POWERGLIDE TRANSMISSION): Overhead-valve. Cast-iron block. Displacement: 235.5 cid. Bore and stroke: 3 $^9/_{16}$ x 3 $^{15}/_{16}$. Compression ratio: 7.5:1. Brake hp: 125 at 4000 rpm. Four main bearings. Hydraulic valve lifters. Included transmission oil cooler, new high-lift camshaft, full-pressure lubrication and new aluminum pistons. Cooling system capacity without heater: 16 qt. Crankcase capacity less filter: 5 qt.

CHASSIS: Wheelbase: (all series) 115 in. Overall length: (all passenger cars) 196 $^7/_{16}$ in., (all station wagons) 198 $^{15}/_{16}$ in. Front tread: (all) 56.69 in. Rear tread: (all) 58.75 in. Tires: (convertible with Powerglide) 7.10 x 15 four-ply, (Townsman station wagon) 6.70 x 15 six-ply, (all others) 6.70 x 15 four-ply. Standard rear axle ratio: 3.7:1. Rear axle ratios: 3.70 on standard shift cars, and 3.55 on Powerglides. Fuel capacity: 16 gal. 6-volt electrical system.

OPTIONS: Custom radio push-button. Custom Deluxe radio. Recirculating heater and defroster (under dash type). Air Flow heater and defroster (dashboard type). E-Z-Eye tinted glass. Autronic Eye automatic headlamp dimmer. Directional signals. Back-up lights. Bumper guards (second pair, front or rear). Front fender gravel shields. Door handle shields. Windshield sunshade (visor). Full wheel discs. Accessory "bird-type" hood ornament. Fender skirts on 150 models. License plate frame. Front and rear bumper tip guards. Stem-wind clock on 150 models. Radio antenna. Locking gas filler door. Ventipane wind deflectors. Left-hand outside rearview mirror. Fog lights. Traffic light viewer. Tissue dispenser. Vacuumatic ashtray. Non-glare rearview mirror. No-Mar fuel door trim. Under-hood light. San-Toy seat covers. Powerglide ($178). Power brakes ($38). Power operated front window lifts ($86). Power operated seat ($86). Power steering ($135). White sidewall tires ($27 exchange).

HISTORICAL FOOTNOTES: New models were introduced in December 1953. Model-year sales totaled 1,151,486. Calendar-year sales reached 1,414,352.

The new 1954 Chevrolet Bel Air Sport Coupe. With three great series, Chevrolet offers the most beautiful choice of models in its field.

How the new Chevrolet wrings more <u>power</u> and more <u>miles</u> out of every gallon of gas . . .

You see a couple of things in our picture up there that combine to make mighty fine motoring—the New England countryside and the new 1954 Chevrolet.

THERE HAS NEVER BEEN a Chevrolet that responded so quickly, smoothly and quietly to your foot on the accelerator. You accelerate, climb hills and whisper along the highway as you never did before.

NEW HIGH-COMPRESSION POWER is the reason behind these important advantages. Chevrolet has the *highest* compression ratio in any leading low-priced car. And high-compression is the key to another very important fact about Chevrolet performance.

IT'S A LONG WAY FROM "FULL" TO "EMPTY." Higher compression means simply that the fuel mixture is squeezed more tightly in the engine to get more power and more work out of the same amount of gas. That is why the Chevrolet gas gauge takes such a long time and so many miles to move from "full" to "empty."

No other low-priced car offers you so many important advantages of high-priced cars, including all the automatic features and controls you could want. Yet, *Chevrolet is the lowest-priced line in the low-price field.* See your Chevrolet dealer. . . . Chevrolet Division of General Motors, Detroit 2, Michigan.

MORE PEOPLE BUY CHEVROLETS THAN ANY OTHER CAR!

SYMBOL OF SAVINGS
CHEVROLET
EMBLEM OF EXCELLENCE

Desert Sunshine by Palm Springs · *Hat and Stole by* Mr. John · *Convertible by* Chevrolet · *Body by* Fisher

Miles-ahead style! Exclusively yours in Bodies by Fisher — whose rightness of fit and ruggedness of build bespeak the extra millions of dollars expended on new production techniques! For sheer beauty of design, safety and enduring value, you're investing wisely when you choose a car with — Body by Fisher.

"Be careful . . . drive safely"

on GM cars only: **CHEVROLET · PONTIAC · OLDSMOBILE · BUICK · CADILLAC**

THE 1954 CHEVROLET

The Bel Air 4-Door Sedan

Far and away the most distinctive and beautiful 4-door sedan in the low-price field. Note the smart new front- and rear-end styling . . . the one-piece curved windshield . . . the huge panoramic rear window. The striking new wheel covers are standard equipment on all Bel Air models.

4

The Bel Air Sport Coupe

It's lively, lovely and luxurious—more beautiful than ever both inside and out! Smart new fabrics and vinyls are combined in the dashing two-tone interior. And it's color-keyed, of course, to harmonize completely with any of the sparkling "fashion fiesta" exterior colors you select. Here's real sports-car flair with all the snug and solid comfort of a sedan.

8

This is how Chevrolet presented its models from the top trim-level Bel Airs, down through the 210s, and on down to the economy-class 150s.

CHAPTER 6

The Bel Air convertible was touted as Chevrolet's most exciting model for its all-new 1955 lineup. The new V-8 engine was exciting for Chevrolet in 1955, but not all Chevrolets had V-8s. Many Chevrolet buyers elected to stick with the proven, efficient six-cylinder engine. V-8 models had small V-8 logos under both tail lights, while six-cylinder cars were blank under the tail lights.

1955

Introduction The 1955 Chevrolet was an all-new car from stem to stern. A new front-end design featured a cellular grille, hooded headlights, redesigned bumpers, new parking lights and a restyled hood ornament. All models featured new wraparound windshields and Contour Cut "dip-down beltlines," as Chevrolet sale literature put it. The dip-down beltline actually appeared on the 1953 Buick Wildcat I Motorama concept car and emerged on production Buicks in 1954. With the disappearance of the rear fender bulge, there were no prewar elements left on the '55 Chevrolet.

The new V-8 sparked one of Chevrolet's best years ever. Some Chevrolet dealers set sales records in 1955 that still stand. Note the add-on oil filter. Chevrolet added a built-in oil filter on the 283 V-8 in 1957.

Other new style features included redesigned parking lights and tail lights, a new side chrome treatment on Bel Airs, and a very plain but attractive rectangular grille with a fine mesh patters with no more garish teeth.

New under the hood was Chevrolet's first V-8 engine since 1918. This compact, overhead-valve V-8 had an over-square design that meant less piston travel, less friction and less wear with horsepower ratings up to 180 when an optional "Power Pack" was ordered. The V-8 could even be had in the base-model 150 as an option. All V-8 Chevrolets had little "V-8" emblems below both tail lights, while six-cylinder cars were blank.

Other new-for-1955 features included tubeless tires, a ball-joint front suspension, Anti-Dive braking, Ball-Race steering, suspended brake and clutch pedals, high-level ventilation, push-button door handles and an open drive shaft taking the place of the old enclosed unit. Hidden inside the body of two-door sedans, four-door sedans, and station wagons was a built-in roll bar in the roof that made the '55 Chevrolet much safer in a roll-over accident.

Long-standing dealers remember the 1955 announcement day with special fondness. Chap Morris Sr. of William L. Morris Chevrolet in Fillmore, California, was among the dealers thrilled with the 1955 Chevrolet.

"We were losing market quickly to Ford (in 1954) because they had a V-8, and they emphasized power and speed, which was what the public wanted," Morris recalls. "In '55, Chevrolet came out with the 265 V-8. Fillmore was a town of about 4,000 people, and we must have had 2,000 people in over the weekend. We had a Bel Air four-door demonstrator. We put over 200 miles on the car in one day driving a mile-and-a-half out of town and back. People were lined up to ride in it. After the presentation in the showroom, you took them out and let them drive it, and when you punched it, it moved, and you could see the stars in their eyes. When you got back to the dealership, we showed them the features album with the different colors available, and it sold itself. That was a great announcement day!"

Dealers also report that, for the first couple of years, Chevrolet's new V-8 used more oil than it should have and lacked a built-in oil filter. Problems with breaking rocker arm studs and premature timing chain wear would be addressed over the following decade.

The Corvette didn't change much from the previous year, but you could get a V-8 in your roadster if you wanted it. Only about 700 'Vettes were built.

I.D. NUMBERS: Serial numbers were stamped on a plate on the left front door hinge pillar. The first symbol in the serial number indicated the model and series: A=One-Fifty 1500 series, B=Two-Ten 2100 series, C=Bel Air 2400 series. E=Corvette 2934 series. The second and third symbols indicated the model year: 55=1955. The fourth symbol indicates the assembly plant as follows: (A) Atlanta, Georgia, (B) Baltimore, Maryland, (F) Flint, Michigan, (J) Janesville, Wisconsin, (K) Kansas City, Missouri, (L) Los Angeles, California, (N) Norwood, Ohio, (O) Oakland, California, (S) St. Louis, Missouri and (T) Tarrytown, New York. The last six symbols are the production sequence number in the specific factory. The beginning serial number for the 1955 150 series was: A55-001001 (six-cylinder) and VA55-001001 (V-8). The beginning serial number for the 1955 210 series was: B55-001001 (six-cylinder) and VB55-001001 (V-8). The beginning serial number for the 1955 Bel Air series was: C55-001001 (six-cylinder) and VC55-001001 (V-8). Corvettes were numbered VE55S001001 to VE55S001700. Engine numbers were stamped on the right side of block near the fuel pump. Six-cylinder engine numbers began 01001-55Z and up. V-8 engine numbers began at 01001-55G and up. It should be noted that engine numbers consisted of four to seven numbers with a prefix or suffix. The prefix or suffix indicated year, engine size, factory, type of valve lifter, and other peculiarities. Restorers can consult Chevrolet shop manuals or master parts catalogs for this type of information. The Fisher Body number plate on the right-hand side of the cowl gives additional information such as the body style number (see second column in tables below), the body production sequence number, the trim (upholstery) number code, and the paint number code.

The 1955 Bel Air two-door sedan. (Fred Lossman)

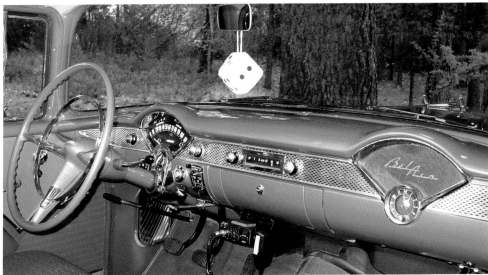

Today's collectors think of the Bel Air two-door hardtop as one of the more collectible of the 1955 Chevrolet lineup, but this Bel Air two-door sedan offers an invisible advantage over the hardtop. All Chevrolet sedans and wagons had a hidden roll bar in the roof that ran across the top from pillar to pillar.

(Fred Lossman)

PAINT COLORS: Monotone paint colors for 1955 were: No. 585 Oynx Black, No. 586 Sea Mist Green, No. 587 Neptune Green, No. 588 Skyline Blue, No. 589 Glacier Blue, No. 590 Copper Maroon, No. 591 Shoireline Beige, No. 592 Autumn Bronze, No. 593 India Ivory, No. 594 Shadow Gray, No. 596 Gypsy Red, No. 598 Regal Turquoise, No. 626 Coral, No. 630 Harvest Gold, and No. 683 Cashmere Blue. Two-tone color combinations for 1955 were: No. 599 Sea Mist Green/Neptune Green, No. 600 Skyline Blue/Glacier Blue, No. 601 Neptune Green/Shoreline Beige, No. 602 India Ivory/Skyline Blue, No. 603 Autumn Bronze/Shoreline Beige, No. 604 Neptune Green/Sea Mist Green, No. 605 India Ivory/Sea Mist Green, No. 606 Shoreline Beige/Autumn Bronze, No. 607 Glacier Blue/Shoreline Beige, No. 608 India Ivory/Oynx Black, No. 610 Glacier Blue/Skyline Blue, No. 612 India Ivory/Regal Turquoise, No. 613 Shoreline Beige/Neptune Green, No. 614 Shoreline Beige/Glacier Blue, No. 615 Shoreline Beige/Gypsy Red, No. 617 India Ivory/Gypsy Red, No. 624 India Ivory/Shadow Gray, No. 627 Shadow Gray/Coral, No. 628 Oynx Black/India Ivory, No. 629 India Ivory/Coral, No. 631 India Ivory/Harvest Gold, No. 682 India Ivory/Cashmere Blue, No. 684 India Ivory/Navajo Tan, and No. 685 India Ivory/Dusk Rose.

Chevrolet's V-8 was the big news for 1955, but many buyers opted for the proven six-cylinder engine which was more than capable of slapping the Chevrolet up to highway speed in ordinary driving.

ONE-FIFTY—SERIES 1500 A: The 150 series was Chevrolet's lowest-priced line. Standard equipment included rubber floor mats front and rear, full-width, all-steel seat frames with "S" springs, all-vinyl upholstery for station wagon and one-piece wraparound windshield. Exterior bright metal decoration was limited to a Chevrolet script on front fender and standard chrome-plated bumpers, grille, door handles, hood ornament, lamp rims and wheel hub center caps.

ONE-FIFTY — SERIES 1500 A

ONE-FIFTY SERIES SIX-CYL

Model No.	Body/Style No.	Body Type & Seating	Factory Price	Shipping Weight	Production Total
1503	55-1219	4d Sed-6P	$1,726	3,165 lbs.	29,898
1502	55-1211	2d Sed-6P	$1,685	3,110 lbs.	66,416
1512	55-1211B	2d Sed-3P	$1,593	3,065 lbs.	11,196
1529	55-1263F	2d Sta Wag-6P	$2,030	3,290 lbs.	17,936

ONE-FIFTY SERIES V-8

Model No.	Body/Style No.	Body Type & Seating	Factory Price	Shipping Weight	Production Total
1503	55-1219	4d Sed-6P	$1,827	3,135 lbs.	—
1502	55-1211	2d Sed-6P	$1,784	3,080 lbs.	—
1512	55-1211B	2d Sed-3P	$1,692	3,055 lbs.	—
1529	55-1263F	2d Sta Wag-6P	$2,129	3,260 lbs.	—

NOTE: *Production totals reflect combined six-cylinder and V-8 production for each body style.*

The sporty 1955 Chevrolet Nomad station wagon was one of the most successful experimental body designs in Chevrolet history. It was unusual without being weird, and it was beautiful without being useless.

TWO-TEN—SERIES 2100 B: The 210 series was Chevrolet's middle-priced line. Standard equipment included all 150 equipment listed above, plus stainless-steel windshield and backlight reveals, chrome front seat and sidewall moldings, glove compartment light, ash trays, cigarette lighter, armrests and assist straps. Additional exterior bright metal decorations included upper beltline and rear fender side and sash moldings.

TWO-TEN SERIES

TWO-TEN SERIES SIX-CYL

Model No.	Body/Style No.	Body Type & Seating	Factory Price	Shipping Weight	Production Total
2103	55-1019	4d Sed-6P	$1,819	3,180 lbs.	317,724
2102	55-1011	2d Sed-6P	$1,775	3,145 lbs.	249,105
2124	55-1011A	2d Clb Cpe-6P	$1,635	3,145 lbs.	115,584
2154	55-1037F	2d Spt Cpe-6P	$1,959	3,172 lbs.	11,675
2129	55-1063F	2d Sta Wag-6P	$2,079	3,330 lbs.	29,916
2109	55-1062F	4d Sta Wag-6P	$2,127	3,370 lbs.	62,303

TWO-TEN SERIES V-8

Model No.	Body/Style No.	Body Type & Seating	Factory Price	Shipping Weight	Production Total
2103	55-1019	4d Sed-6P	$1,918	3,150 lbs.	—
2102	55-1011	2d Sed-6P	$1,674	3,125 lbs.	—
2124	55-1011A	2d Clb Cpe-6P	$1,934	3,115 lbs.	—
2154	55-1037F	2d Spt Cpe-6P	$2,058	3,144 lbs.	—
2129	55-1063F	2d Sta Wag-6P	$2,176	3,300 lbs.	—
2109	55-1062F	4d Sta Wag-6P	$2,226	3,340 lbs.	—

NOTE: Production totals reflect combined six-cylinder and V-8 production for each body style.

BEL AIR—SERIES 2400 C: The Bel Air was Chevrolet's top series. Standard equipment included most features found on the lower priced lines, plus carpets on closed body styles, chrome-ribbed headliner on the sport coupe, richer upholstery fabrics, horizontal chrome strip on sides of front fender and doors, narrow white-painted insert on rear fender horizontal side molding, gold Bel Air script and Chevrolet crest behind slanting vertical sash molding, ribbed vertical trim plate on sides above rear bumper ends, wide chrome window and door post reveals, and full wheel discs.

BEL AIR SERIES 2400 C

BEL AIR SERIES SIX-CYL

Model No.	Body/Style No.	Body Type & Seating	Factory Price	Shipping Weight	Production Total
2403	55-1019D	4d Sed-6P	$1,932	3,200 lbs.	345,372
2402	55-1011D	2d Sed-6P	$1,668	3,155 lbs.	168,313
2454	55-1037D	2d HT-6P	$2,067	3,195 lbs.	185,562
2434	55-1067D	2d Conv-5P	$2,206	3,315 lbs.	41,292
2429	55-1064DF	2d Nomad Wag-6P	$2,472	3,300 lbs.	6,103
2409	55-1062DF	4d Sta Wag-6P	$2,262	3,385 lbs.	2,313

BEL AIR SERIES V-8

Model No.	Body/Style No.	Body Type & Seating	Factory Price	Shipping Weight	Production Total
2403	55-1019D	4d Sed-6P	$2,031	3,170 lbs.	—
2402	55-1011D	2d Sed-6P	$1,987	3,125 lbs.	—
2454	55-1037D	2d HT-6P	$2,166	3,165 lbs.	—
2434	55-1067D	2d Conv-5P	$2,305	3,285 lbs.	—
2429	55-1064DF	2d Nomad Wag-6P	$2,571	3270 lbs.	—
2409	55-1062DF	4d Sta Wag-6P	$2,361	3,355 lbs.	—

NOTE: *Production totals reflect combined six-cylinder and V-8 production for each body style.*

This Nomad is extra-special. It came from the factory with air-conditioning and power brakes. All the original equipment is visible in the engine compartment, and the outlets for the air-conditioning are at the ends of the dash.

Ford and Plymouth had both produced two-door station wagons by 1955, but nothing as sporty as the Nomad.

The Nomad was still a practical car, and the interior was roomy, made of tough materials, and could be used as a full-duty station wagon.

Only 700 1955 Corvettes were built.

CORVETTE—(SIX-CYL/V-8)—SERIES 2934 E: Corvette styling remained the same as last year's model. The big news was the availability of a V-8 engine. An enlarged gold "V" within the word "CheVrolet" on the front fenders was a quick way to tell the V-8 powered (12-volt electrical system) cars from those with a six-cylinder engine (and six-volt electrical system). On the 1955 V-8 cars the frame was modified to allow room for the fuel pump.

CORVETTE SERIES

CORVETTE SERIES SIX-CYL

Model No.	Body/Style No.	Body Type & Seating	Factory Price	Shipping Weight	Production Total
2934	2934	2-dr Rds-2P	2,774	2,705 lbs.	Note 1

CORVETTE SERIES V-8

2934	2934	2-dr Rds-2P	2,909	2,870 lbs.	Note 1

NOTE 1: *Total production of both models was 700. At least a half dozen six-cylinder Corvettes were built as 1955 models.*

ENGINES:

ALL SERIES STANDARD SIX-CYL (MANUAL TRANSMISSION): Overhead-valve. Cast-iron block. Displacement: 235.5 cid. Bore and stroke: 3 $^9/_{16}$ x 3 $^{15}/_{16}$. Compression ratio: 7.5:1. Brake hp: 123 at 3800 rpm. Taxable hp: 30.40. Torque: 207 lbs.-ft. at 2000 rpm. Four main bearings. Solid valve lifters. Carburetor: Rochester one-barrel "B" type. Cooling system capacity without heater: 16 qt. Crankcase capacity (less filter): 5 qt.

ALL SERIES STANDARD SIX-CYL (POWERGLIDE TRANSMISSION): Overhead-valve. Cast-iron block. Displacement: 235.5 cid. Bore and stroke: 3 $^9/_{16}$ x 3 $^{15}/_{16}$. Compression ratio: 7.5:1. Brake hp: 136 at 4200 rpm. Taxable hp: 30.40. Torque: 209 lbs.-ft. at 2200 rpm. Four main bearings. Hydraulic valve lifters. Carburetor: Rochester one-barrel Model 7007181. Include transmission oil cooler, new high-lift camshaft, full-pressure lubrication, new aluminum pistons. (Standard with Powerglide and available in all car lines.) Cooling system capacity without heater: 16 qt. Crankcase capacity (less filter): 5 qt.

This 1955 Chevrolet Nomad came with factory air-conditioning, power steering and power brakes. Typical of most American cars in the 1950s, the power steering pump was mounted to the back of the generator.

TURBO-FIRE BASE V-8: Overhead-valve. Cast-iron block and head. Bore and stroke: 3.75 x 3.00 in. Displacement: 265 cid. Compression ratio: 8.0:1. Brake hp: 162 at 4400 rpm. Taxable hp: 45.0. Torque: 257 lbs.-ft. at 2200. Five main bearings. Hydraulic valve lifters. Crankcase capacity: 4 qt. (add 1 qt. for new filter). Cooling system capacity: 16 qt. (add 1 qt. for heater). Carburetor: Rochester 2 BC two-barrel. Engine codes: G, GC, GF, GG, GJ, GK, F, or FC.

TURBO-FIRE OPTIONAL V-8: Overhead-valve. Cast-iron block and head. Bore and stroke: 3.75 x 3.00 in. Displacement: 265 cid. Compression ratio: 8.0:1. Brake hp: 180 lbs.-ft. at 4600 rpm. Taxable hp: 45.0. Torque: 260 at 2800. Five main bearings. Hydraulic valve lifters. Crankcase capacity: 4 qt. (add 1 qt. for new filter). Cooling system capacity: 16 qt. (add 1 qt. for heater). Carburetor: Rochester four-barrel. Engine codes: GD, GE, GL, or GM.

CHASSIS: Wheelbase: 115 in. Overall length: (passenger cars) 195.6 in., (station wagons) 197.1 in. Front tread: 58 in. Rear tread: 58.8 in. Tires: 6.70 x 15 tubeless. Fuel tank capacity: 16 gal. 12-volt electrical system. **Corvette chassis:** Wheelbase: 102 inches. Overall length: 167 inches. Front tread: 57 inches. Rear tread: 58.8 inches. Tires: 6.70 x 15. Front suspension: Coil springs, tube shocks and stabilizer bar. Rear suspension: Leaf springs, tube shocks and solid rear axle. Drum brakes. Steel disk wheels. Axle ratio: 3.55:1.

OPTIONS: A three-speed manual gearbox with column-mounted gearshift was standard on all models. Overdrive was available on the manual transmission at $108 extra. Powerglide two-speed automatic transmission was available at $178 extra. The V-8 engine was available with an optional "power-pack" that included single four-barrel carburetor and dual exhaust. Optional horsepower rating with "'power-pack" was 180 at 4600 rpm. Power steering ($92). Power brakes ($38). Directional signals. Electric windshield wipers. Power windows. Power seat. Heater and defroster. Air conditioning. White sidewall tires. Fender antenna. Locking gas cap. Continental tire kit. Outside sun visor. Self de-icing wiper blades. Wiring junction block. Electric clock. Compass. Seat covers. Accelerator pedal cover. Wire wheel covers. Tissue dispenser. Exhaust extension. Filter and element. License plate frame. Glare-shields. Grille guard. Fender guard. Door edge guard. Gasoline filler guard. Tool kit. Back-up lamps. Courtesy lamps. Cigarette lighter. Floor mats. Outside rearview mirrors. Inside non-glare rearview mirrors. Vanity visor. Manual radio. Push-button radio. Signal-seeking radio. Automatic top riser armrests. Wheel trim rings. Safety light with mirror. Sport lamp. Electric shaver. Parking brake signal. Door handle shields. Front fender shields. Rear speaker. Vent shades. Inside sun visor. Traffic light viewer. Foot-operated windshield washer. Vacuum-operated windshield washer.

HISTORICAL FOOTNOTES: Model year production totaled ,1702,710 units. Body style 55-1211B was a utility sedan. Body style 55-1263F was a two-door Handyman station wagon. Body style 55-1062F was a four-door Handyman station wagon. Body style 55-1063F was a Townsman station wagon. Body style 55-1011A was the Del Ray. Body style 55-1037F was a midyear model. Body style 55-1062DF was the Beauville station wagon. Body style 55-1064DF was the Nomad, a two-door station wagon with special hardtop styling, introduced as a midyear model.

THE BEL AIR 4-DOOR SEDAN in Autumn Bronze. Chevrolet's new Fisher Body combines that long, low, "let's go" look with more room inside for hips, hats and shoulders, and new rigidity and safety underneath. It's one more reason why Chevrolet's stealing the thunder from the high-priced cars!

THE BEL AIR SPORT COUPE in Shadow Gray and Coral. You ought to see how the *interior* looks, too!

THE CONVERTIBLE in Shoreline Beige and Gypsy Red. Top, interior and exterior colors all harmonize.

THE BEL AIR BEAUVILLE in Regal Turquoise. Both rear seat backrest and cushion fold flat for extra cargo space.

THE DELRAY CLUB COUPE in India Ivory over Harvest Gold. The interior's all-vinyl—practical, washable, colorful.

THE "TWO-TEN" HANDYMAN in Shoreline Beige over Glacier Blue. Another handsome and durable all-vinyl interior.

THE "ONE-FIFTY" 4-DOOR SEDAN in Shoreline Beige. The seeing's better through that Sweep-Sight windshield.

THE *motoramic* **CHEVROLET**

THE "TWO-TEN" 4-DOOR SEDAN

THE "TWO-TEN" DELRAY CLUB COUPE

THE "TWO-TEN" 2-DOOR STATION WAGON

THE "TWO-TEN" 4-DOOR STATION WAGON

The "Two-Ten" Handyman.

Never have you seen Station Wagons as wonderful as the new Chevrolets!

You can have your cake and eat it. too—with Chevrolet's spanking-new line of Station Wagons! For here is sophisticated big-city style (and the longest look of any Chevrolet) . . . plus pack-horse performance and astonishing new utility features. Now, both the rear seat cushion and the backrest fold flush with the floor to give almost 11 inches more cargo space. Curved rear quarter windows combine with the deep Sweep-Sight Windshield to give visibility unlimited. With this two-in-one versatility you get all of Chevrolet's great engineering advances—the 162-h.p. "Turbo-Fire V8" or the two new "Blue-Flame" 6's, the smoothness of Glide-Ride front suspension, the stability of outrigger rear springs, Anti-Dive braking control, 12-volt electrical system and new Synchro-Mesh transmission. Plus your choice of extra-cost options such as Powerglide automatic transmission or Overdrive, Power Steering, Power Brakes—even Air Conditioning (on V8 models). How versatile can a car be? Why not call your Chevrolet dealer and see? . . . Chevrolet Division of General Motors, Detroit 2, Michigan.

More than a new car *a new* ***concept*** *of low-cost motoring*

1955 Announcement Day

(Dick Romm)

A Hot Day

Pat Matlach heard rumbles from friends in the car business that something new was coming from Chevrolet for 1955. Matlach was still in his 20s and a successful used-car dealer in Victorville, California, on the curbs of Route 66. Fifty years later, Matlach's Desert Motors still has the highway in front and the Santa Fe railroad tracks in back that it had in 1955.

"A train full of new Chevrolets stopped in back of my car lot and sat there for a while," Matlach remembers. "We went out there and peeked at them sitting on the train, and the first '55 Chevrolet I saw was one of those that had that beautiful salmon and silver two-tone paint. It was gorgeous, but it was on the bottom of the train car with another Chevrolet above it, and it had oil all over it that had dripped from the one above, but that was a normal occurrence during shipping in those days."

Seeing the all-new 1955 Chevrolet on the train means Matlach saw it before some actual Chevrolet dealership employees did.

Many veteran car dealers remember announcement days fondly—when curtains hung in the showroom windows, cars arrived on trucks all covered up, cryptic advertisements piqued curiosity, and the final unveiling drew crowds of excited, curious potential customers.

During the post-World War II boom, even economy car buyers wanted something more. Ford had been putting V-8s in the common people's hands since 1932, but the overheating Ford flathead V-8 had outlived its advantages by 1949, when the Oldsmobile Rocket 88 brought a much more advanced V-8 into an accessible price range for the average person. Some sources hold up 1953 as the first year V-8s outsold six-cylinder engines, and by 1954, Chevrolet and Plymouth were working hard to catch up to Ford, which had finally replaced the antiquated flathead with a much more advanced overhead-valve V-8. Studebaker's sales did not even approach Chevrolet's, but probably should have, because the Studebakers had a lot a of style and their V-8 engine was moderately priced and gaining a good reputation.

(Dick Romm)

(Dick Romm)

Dealers, Demonstrators, and Dreams

The dealerships went wild. Crowds jammed the showrooms, the demonstrators never cooled off, and some dealerships partied until midnight. The 1955 Chevrolet had snap, style, and quality, and it all coincided with a great year for car sales in general. Some existing Chevrolet dealerships set records in 1955 that still stand.

Jim Applegate was in the heart of the action. Flint, Michigan, is a GM town. GM cars are made there, driven there, and remembered there. Applegate Chevrolet had a hit on its hands in 1955.

"It was a very exciting day. It was an exciting car, really," Applegate remembers. "I remember a red two-tone convertible with the red and tan combination. The styling was excellent. It was a huge breakthrough from 1954. The '54 was high and narrow, and the '55 was low and wide with the V-8 engine. The whole thing was huge. We ran out of the '54s, so we had an empty showroom for about a week with no cars to sell. The new '55s were covered with canvas, and when we opened up the showroom on announcement day, it was a four-day event. We were here until midnight every night. The place was just jammed. It was probably the biggest announcement we ever had.

"Ed Cole had the best talent in the automotive business at that time under his guidance. They tested out the V-8 with the Michigan State Police, and they tested it out for a year in some '54 Chevrolets. Chevrolet was a team of its own at that time, unlike now, when things are shared through the whole corporation. The head of Chevrolet had a lot of input into the process as to how the car was going to look. Today, the car comes in and nobody knows it, but back then, they peaked right up

Chevrolet and Plymouth both got V-8s in 1955. Plymouth's V-8 was of polyspheric design and a close relative to Chrysler's hemispheric V-8s. It's arguable the Plymouth and Dodge V-8s were much more proven, advanced, and of higher quality than Chevrolet's 1955 V-8, but no other company matched General Motors in creating excitement. Nothing was more important in 1950s America than being modern, and the 1955 Chevrolet was modern all the way through, not just under the hood. The rear fender bulges that Chevrolet wore through the 1954 season were the last shadows of the prewar era when rear fenders were bolted on. The 1955 Chevrolet had absolutely no bulge to its rear fenders, and at last, there was no hint of a stagecoach lurking under the skin of this automobile. Rear fender bulges had disappeared from Ford in 1949 and Plymouth in 1953.

to a specific date, and you usually got enough sales just from the announcement day to get you through to the end of the year."

Applegate is able to back up the 1955 Chevrolet's success with numbers. Applegate Chevrolet sold 2,950 new cars and trucks in 1954, but sales shot up to 4,518 for 1955. Sales fell below the 1954 totals in the next coupe of years with better times coming to Applegate again in the 1960s.

Fillmore, California, is a small farming town surrounded by orange orchards and sometimes shrouded in fog off the Pacific Ocean. William L. Morris opened his Chevrolet dealership on October 29, 1929—the day the stock market crashed and sent the country into the Great Depression. Morris' dealership survived obeying the principles of Chevrolet's Quality Dealer Program in the 1930s, and Bill Morris would go out every morning with a hotshot battery and a big coffee pot to start all the farmers' tractors for them. The farmers became loyal customers, and 25 years later, his son, Chap Morris Sr., was at his father's side for the 1955 announcement day.

"The last year we had a six-only was 1954, and we were losing market quickly to Ford because they had a V-8, and they emphasized power and speed, which was what the public wanted," Chap Morris Sr. explains. "In '55, Chevrolet came out with the 265 V-8. Fillmore was a town of about 4,000 people, and we must have had 2,000 people in over the weekend. We had a Bel Air four-door demonstrator. We put over 200 miles on the car in one day driving a mile-and-a-half out of town and back. People were lined up to ride in it. After the presentation in the showroom, you took them out and let them drive it, and when you punched it, it moved, and you could see the stars in their eyes. When you got back to the dealership, we showed them the features album with the different colors available, and it sold itself. That was a great announcement day. We had all types of giveaways—yard sticks, bottle openers, balloons, refreshments for the crowd and an exciting new product. The public was ready for that."

Dick Stowers was already a seasoned Chevrolet salesman by 1955, having worked for his father in-law, Frank Culberson, for several years. Culberson Chevrolet sold bowtie products in Pampa, Texas, in the heart of the panhandle's oil/natural gas/cattle country. Stowers enjoyed selling early Powerglide Chevrolets to economy-car buyers because the Powerglide cars' higher-speed rear axle ratios gave them expensive-car performance for the long drives between towns on the flat Pandandle prairies. When the V-8 settled in front of the Powerglide, times were good at Culberson Chevrolet.

"Announcement days were a headache, but I enjoyed it, and I wish we'd get back to it," Stowers reminisces. "Today, we've got several lines with GM at the same

(Dick Romm)

dealership in Hales Corners, Wisconsin, southwest of Milwaukee. Holz Motors entered the 21st century as the highest-selling car dealership of any brand in the state of Wisconsin, but in 1955, the dealership still only had room for three cars in its showroom.

"The big highlight of 1955 was the first V-8 we had," Jerry Holz tells. "We really had something to talk about and sell. Everyone had V-8s but us by then. You have to remember that it was a completely new model, and it was a good-looking car. The cars came on the carrier covered, and we kept them under cover. We really had a new model to talk about. It's wasn't just a change in serial number, it was a real change in the car. The whole thing was cool! We had a nice yellow convertible with kind of a green interior, and it was a cool car. My nephew still talks about it because he was in high school and going to the prom, and I let him use it. It might not sound too smart, but it was such a cool car that I let him take it. We went from the old stovebolt six to a V-8, which was brand new for us, and it was a great engine. (The racers started) using them in dirt track racing at that time, and it was very popular to be racing those cars. Chevrolet finally had a car that would compete, and it was really important for the image of the company and sales. In those days, the car companies were run by car guys, not accountants. We didn't really try and sell cars at the announcement. If someone really wanted one, we'd sell it, but it was mostly party time."

Legacy

The 1955 announcement day was one of Chevrolet's finest hours. The new V-8 was exciting, but that wasn't all there was to a '55 Chevrolet. Fred Lossman, of Nevada City, California, proudly drives his six-cylinder 1955 Chevrolet Bel Air on the northern California back roads and likes to remind other car enthusiasts that Chevrolet sold hundreds of thousands of six-cylinder Chevrolets in 1955. The proven, reliable six didn't meet any skepticism from traditional Chevrolet buyers and was important for sales for its familiarity and trustworthy nature. Even a six-cylinder Chevrolet was a much more exciting car than it had been only a year before and had much to say about the rapid unfolding of the Jet Age. The V-8s were quicker, but they weren't that much bigger in volume than the sixes, and a six-cylinder Chevrolet didn't hold up traffic, either.

Whether a six-cylinder 210 sedan or a dolled-up V-8 Bel Air hardtop, Chevrolet offered up its dealers and customers its most exciting announcement day ever in 1955.

time, and we usually have cars from two or three model years on the new car lots at all times. I kind of miss the days when we could cover up the windows, and everyone knew the new cars were coming. We used to unload the new cars off the railroad cars at night. We'd have them all ready to go, and all we had to do was drive them out of the boxcar. It was only about three blocks. Our other problem was trying to get them serviced and ready to sell without people seeing them. We had to put the hubcaps on them, make sure all the fluid levels were up and the belts were properly tight, and wash them before we could put them on the lot or sell them. Those were fun days—days that made you stay in the business. I don't think I'll ever forget when we had the new car show in for the 1955 model in the fall of 1954. We had the windows all covered up. We had a brand new '55 Chevrolet in the showroom--green with a tan top. It was the first one with the V-8, all that radically curved glass, and (all those new convenience options). It was a pretty car. Somebody threw a piece of pig lead through the plate glass window and hit the hood and broke the windshield. It took us five weeks to get the car fixed. I was scared to death of that car because it ran $2,300, and I didn't think we'd ever be able to sell it at that price."

R.W. Holz took on a Chevrolet franchise in 1915, having already handled K.R.I.T and Imperial automobiles. R.W. Holz's son, Jerry, still runs Holz Motors on the same block where his father founded the

Blanck Chevrolet in Brownsburg, Indiana, celebrated the 1955 announcement along with the rest of the Chevrolet world. Here, Edward Blanck Sr. poses with a '55 Nomad. (Blanck family collection))

Three members of the Blanck Chevrolet sales staff show that even the plainest Chevrolet 210 sedan was an exciting new car for 1955. (Blanck family collection)

The 1955 Chevrolet was the first Chevrolet to leave the prewar world completely behind by thoroughly eliminating any hint of a rear fender bulge. The rear fender bulge of 1954 was the last remnant of the prewar world when the rear fenders were bolted onto cars as separate pieces. The 1955 Chevrolet was all-new from the ground up, and stylistically, it was all one piece.

THE BEL AIR 2-DOOR SEDAN

THE BEL AIR CONVERTIBLE

THE BEL AIR 4-DOOR STATION WAGON

THE BEL AIR SPORT COUPE

COPYRIGHT 1954—CHEVROLET MOTOR DIVISION, GENERAL MOTORS CORPORATION

Fingertip Facts for the 1955 Chevrolet

A Pocket-Sized Arsenal for the Chevrolet Salesman

By 1955, General Motors had decades of practice at creating the best automotive imagery in the industry, even for its lowest-priced make, and *Fingertip Facts for the 1955 Chevrolet* was a powerful little weapon in this competitive, record-setting year.

The little book was just the right size to ride in the salesman's coat pocket, and he could whip it out any time a customer made the mistake of challenging Chevrolet's virtues against Ford or Plymouth. Some of the book's information is legitimate and made a strong case for Chevrolet, while other parts of the book will make a true gearhead roll his eyes and smile at Chevrolet's exaggerations. Even at its sillier moments, Fingertip Facts for the 1955 Chevrolet is fun to read and an interesting insight in to the business of selling cars in the mid-'50s.

Ford and Plymouth were all-new for 1955, too, but Chevrolet beat them with beautiful imagery and creative slogans that emphasized modernity. "New when coming, new when passing, new when going!" The Jet Age had not transformed into the Space Age yet, and Chevrolet was still using fun whiz-bang names like Coloramic interiors, Turbofire V-8, and Blue Flame 136.

The illustrations were beautiful, and surprisingly, many of the best illustrations were of the car's mechanical components. The detailed, accurate, exploded views of clutch and transmission assemblies would have been of great interest to the guy who wants to know how his car works, and an artsy diagram of the Powerglide shows—and, yes, exaggerates—its simplicity. One of the book's most impressive illustrations is of the undercarriage from an angle and perspective that legitimately shows the car's new chassis.

Most of the time, hardtops and convertibles are considered to be more "cool" than sedans, but Fingertip Facts for the 1955 Chevrolet shows something that even today's Chevrolet enthusiast can be proud of. Chevrolet four-door sedans, two-door post sedans, and station wagons had a hidden roll bar in the roof that ran from center-post to center-post across the top of the car. A '50s family man with a growing family might have

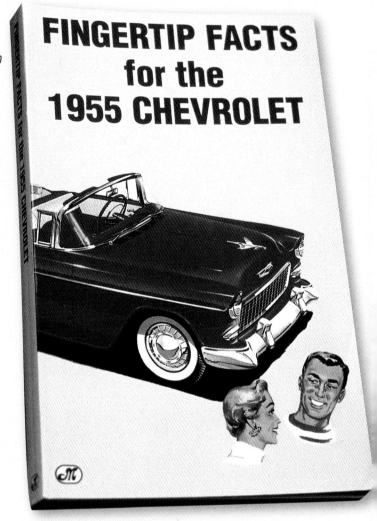

taken this safety feature pretty seriously. The book also makes legitimate arguments about the superior shapes of Chevrolet's glass design compared to Ford and Plymouth, while also making silly claims about superior glass area that only amounted to fractions of an inch here and there.

In the back of "Fingertip Facts for the 1955 Chevrolet," there are several pages of forms in which the dealer could fill out the prices of his Chevrolets versus the local prices of Fords and Plymouths on a side-by-side, model-by-model basis. The Chevrolet dealer could prove he had done his homework and was ready to give the customer the best deal in town.

The General Motors LaSalle II:
Influencing Chevrolet and Corvette Design

1955 LaSalle II

General Motors called it the Motorama—a glittering, gleaming, spectacle that announced the corporation's newest wheeled offerings to the public in Streamline Modern style, reflected in pools of rippling chrome. Through the 1950s, GM quickened the heartbeats of millions of Americans who were looking forward to a shining future, gliding along in high-horsepower luxury on new scientifically designed superhighways. The traveling Motorama shows introduced Mr. and Mrs. America to the practical GM cars available that season, but taking center stage were the dream cars—cars designed purely as art. The Motorama dream cars rarely had functioning engines, doors a person could fit through, or windows that could be seen through safely, but as pure art, they created and experimented with design themes and elements that found their beautiful way onto production cars. One pair of dream cars influenced Chevrolet and Corvette for several years, and their ghosts show through skins of some of America's favorite Chevrolets from the late-1950s.

Looking back, the Jazz Age hit some bumps. The Roaring '20s roared, indeed, but an agricultural crisis and economic slump smacked the United States in 1923, and while the Charleston flapped beaded dresses through the rest of the decade, the auto industry matured out of its maverick beginnings and became serious business. Executives devised strategies to survive future economic slumps, and by the end of the 1920s, four of GM's five divisions had lower-priced companion cars. Buick had the Marquette, and Oldsmobile had the Viking. Oakland's companion car become so popular that it became a GM division all its own—Pontiac.

Another GM companion car is also well remembered for its rather long life and pleasing features. The LaSalle served as Cadillac's companion from 1927 to 1940, and just the name inspires smiles from those lucky enough to have owned them. Their looks rivaled the Cadillac with tall, sleek, slender grilles; lighter, quicker, more nimble construction; and, by the late-1930s, large, silent V-8 engines and perfectly-geared transmissions that made

The LaSalle served as Cadillac's companion from 1927 to 1940, and just the name inspires smiles from those lucky enough to have owned them.

them some of the best-performing production cars on the road. LaSalles were set apart from Cadillacs by their plain-Jane interiors, but they weren't set apart enough from Buicks. GM felt the LaSalle competed with Buick, and the mighty LaSalle said goodbye.

World War II passed, and America settled into the tranquil but exciting rhythms of postwar prosperity. The public wanted more from their cars than just transportation. The time was right for GM to bring out a specialty car. GM stylist Henry Lauve once said a Fiat sports car influenced him while he visited European design houses and fashion shows looking for clues to what trends GM's future styling should follow, and he contributed some of these influences to the 1953 Corvette's design. The Corvette was a smash when it appeared in its first Motorama show, and in spite of its limited production totals and completely ordinary six-cylinder drive train, the 1953 and '54 Corvettes foretold the Corvette's place in the American specialty-car market. Throughout its history, the Corvette has only captured about 2-4 percent of Chevrolet sales, but many consider it America's sports car, and that reputation became deserved when the Corvette went V-8 in 1955. One 1955 Motorama concept car brought the production Corvette one of its most memorable design elements.

According to Joe Bortz, a leading collector of American dream cars, GM stylist Harley Earl felt compelled to resurrect the LaSalle name for a pair of elegant, mature sports cars destined for the Motorama turntables of 1955—a small but stately four-door hardtop, and an aggressively sporty open two-seater that both proudly brandished LaSalle's "LaS" logo from the 1930s. The four-door was painted and upholstered in GM's alluring LeSabre Blue, while the two-seater gleamed a pearlescent white with contrasting side indentations of Bahama Blue. The same minds conceived both cars as two versions of the same car, but the cars' personalities couldn't be more different. The four-door makes a gentleman want to hold the door open for a lady and take her to the opera, but the two-seater wants to blast from a stop in a howl of screaming rubber, leaving a trail of smoke from its open rear wheel wells.

The LaSalle IIs had a certain GM "look" because a number of their design themes appeared on production cars later in the 1950s. The hardtop's roof line appeared on production Cadillac four-door hardtops in 1957 and filtered to the rest of GM's divisions in 1958, and its compound-curve windshield appeared on production GM cars in 1959 and '60. It's easy to think the two-seater looks like a Corvette, when it's really the other way around. The LaSalle II's side indentations and two-toning emerged on Corvettes in 1956 and dressed the little cars through 1962. The Wildcat I also appears to have contributed its windshield to Corvette design through the 1950s.

The LaSalle IIs also foretold the future under the skin with their all-aluminum, fuel-injected, double overhead-cam V-6 engines, independent front and rear suspension, a novel braking system and unit-body construction.

Once they had served their purposes, GM treated its Motorama dream cars very unceremoniously. Joe Bortz found both LaSalle IIs in a junkyard and has given them a loving home along with other GM Motorama dream cars like the '53 Pontiac Parisienne, '64 Pontiac Banshee, and '53 Buick Wildcat I.

America's sports car was a timely, beautiful, and successful creation, but even the Corvette had roots elsewhere and connections not only with GM's Motorama cars from the 1950s but also with one of GM's largest prewar cars—the LaSalle.

CHAPTER 7

For many Corvette enthusiasts, the 1956 styling would never be surpassed.

Introduction

A redesigned full-width grille with large rectangular parking lights, new bumpers and guards (except on wagons), revised side chrome, and new tail lights with the gas filler hidden behind the left-hand light characterized 1956 Chevrolets. New models included a Bel Air four-door hardtop (a.k.a. sports sedan) and nine-passenger station wagons in the 210 and Bel Air lines. Horsepower was increased. Other 1956 selling features included Glide-Ride front suspension, continued anti-dive braking, tubeless tires, Outrigger rear springs, a concealed gas filler behind the tail light, a 12-volt electrical system, new precision-aimed headlights, a new longer-life battery and an automatic choke.

Chevrolet's first four-door hardtop—the 1956 Bel Air sports sedan.

The 1956 Chevrolet was an attractive update from 1955. In trimless, base-model form, a 1955 Chevrolet 150 looked rather unfinished, but the 1956 models looked finished even in base trim. The little bowties all over the dashboard in 1955 disappeared in 1956, leaving smooth, clean, lines sweeping across the chrome dash appliqué.

The Corvette got its first major restyling in '56 with the roadster turning into a convertible with rollup windows and a top that folded down into a well behind the cockpit.

It had all new body panels and a side cove that remained prominent up through 1962. The hood received a pair of parallel bulges. Auxiliary hardtops were also offered for the first time. Tail lights were integrated into the rounded fenders and exhaust exited through the rear bumper.

I.D. NUMBERS: Serial numbers were stamped on a plate on the left front door hinge pillar. The first symbol in the serial number indicated the model and series: A=One-Fifty 1500 series six-cylinder, VA=One-Fifty 1500 series V-8, B=Two-Ten 2100 series six-cylinder, VB=Two-Ten 2100 series V-8, C=Bel Air 2400 series six-cylinder, VC=Bel Air 2400 series V-8. E=Corvette 2934 series. The second and third symbols indicated the model year: 56=1956. The fourth symbol indicates the assembly plant as follows: (A) Atlanta, Georgia, (B) Baltimore, Maryland, (F) Flint, Michigan, (J) Janesville, Wisconsin, (K) Kansas City, Missouri, (L) Los Angeles, California, (N) Norwood, Ohio, (O) Oakland, California, (S) St. Louis, Missouri and (T) Tarrytown, New York. The last six symbols are the production sequence number in the specific factory. Engine numbers were stamped on the right side of block near fuel pump. Six-cylinder engine numbers 01001-56Z to 525227 were used. V-8 engine numbers 01001-56G to 676997 were used. The Fisher Body number plate on the right-hand side of the cowl gives additional information such as the body style number (see second column in tables below), the body production sequence number, the trim (upholstery) number code and the paint number code.

PAINT COLORS: Monotone paint colors for 1956 were: No. 687 Onyx Black, No. 688 Pinecrest Green, No. 690 Sherwood Green, No. 691 Nassau Blue, No. 692 Harbor Blue, No. 693 Dusk Plum, No. 694 India Ivory, No. 695 Crocus Yellow, No. 697 Matador Red, No. 698 Twilight Turquoise, No. 749 Tropical Turquoise, No. 750 Calypso Cream, and No. 752 Inca Silver. Two-tone color combinations were: No. 696 Crocus Yellow/Onyx Black, No. 700 Sierra Gold/Adobe Beige, No. 701 India Ivory/Onyx Black, No. 702 Sherwood Green/Pinecrest Green, No. 703 Harbor Blue/Nassau Blue. No. 705 India Ivory/Pinecrest Green, No. 706 India Ivory/Sherwood Green, No. 707 India Ivory/Nassau Blue, No. 708 India Ivory/Dusk Plum, No. 710 India Ivory/Twilight Turquoise, No. 711 India Ivory/Matador Red, No. 715 Matador Red/Dune Beige, No. 717 Crocus Yellow/Laurel Green, No. 721 India Ivory/Dawn Gray, No. 754 India Ivory/Tropical Turquoise, No. 755 Calypso Cream/Onyx Black, No. 756 Grecian Gold/Calypso Cream, No. 757 Inca Silver/Imperial Ivory, and No. 763 Matador Red/Adobe Beige.

ONE-FIFTY—SERIES 1500 A: The restyling for 1956 Chevrolets included: One-Fifty models had Chevrolet rear fender nameplates, chrome moldings around the windshield and rear window and a horizontal body side molding. This chrome strip ran from just behind the headlamp hood crease line to a point below the rear side window, where it was intersected by a slanting sash molding embossed in windsplit style. Standard equipment included a two-spoke steering wheel with horn ring, lockable glovebox, dome light, and cloth and vinyl upholstery (all-vinyl on station wagons). Features such as the upholstery fabrics or provision of a dashboard ashtray varied per body style, but all had black rubber floor mats and small hubcaps as standard equipment. The 150 only had one inside sun visor on the driver's side.

The 1956 Chevrolet 210 was not fancy, but this one has the optional all-vinyl Del Ray interior package that the working men and mothers liked because they could clean the upholstery with nothing more than a damp cloth. This 210 has full wheel covers instead of the small dog-dish hub caps 210s ordinarily came with.

ONE-FIFTY SERIES 1500 A

ONE-FIFTY SERIES SIX-CYL

Model No.	Body/Style No.	Body Type & Seating	Factory Price	Shipping Weight	Production Total
1503	1219	4d Sed-6P	$1,869	3,206 lbs.	29,898
1502	1211	2d Sed-6P	$1,826	3,164 lbs.	66,416
1512	1211B	2d Utl Sed-3P	$1,734	3,127 lbs.	11,196
1529	1263F	2d Sta Wag-6P	$2,171	3,309 lbs.	17,936

ONE-FIFTY SERIES V-8

Model No.	Body/Style No.	Body Type & Seating	Factory Price	Shipping Weight	Production Total
1503	1219	4d Sed-6P	$1,968	3,186 lbs.	—
1502	1211	2d Sed-6P	$3,164	3,144 lbs.	—
1512	1211B	2d Utl Sed-3P	$1,833	3,107 lbs.	—
1529	1263F	2d Sta Wag-6P	$2,270	3,289 lbs.	—

NOTE: Production totals reflect combined six-cylinder and V-8 production for each body style.

TWO-TEN—SERIES 2100 B: The Two-Ten series was Chevrolet's middle-priced line. These cars also carried Chevrolet rear fender nameplates and had chrome moldings around the windshield, backlight, and windowsills. The side trim was distinctive in that the single horizontal molding swept downward, towards the rear bumper end, from the point where the sash molding intersected it below the rear side window. Exterior and interior details varied per body style, but all models had two sun visors, ashtrays, cigarette lighters, and richer interior trims. The Del Ray coupe featured deep-pile carpets and all-vinyl upholstery, while others had vinyl-coated rubber floor mats with vinyl and cloth trims. A two-spoke steering wheel with horn ring was used. Small hubcaps were standard equipment. Specific interior colors were standard, but custom colored upholstery was optional. A brand-new style was a pillarless four-door hardtop, which was called a sport sedan.

TWO-TEN SERIES 2100 B

Model No.	Body/Style No.	Body Type & Seating	Factory Price	Shipping Weight	Production Total
TWO-TEN SERIES SIX-CYL					
2103	1019	4d Sed-6P	$1,955	3,212 lbs.	283,125
2113	1039	4d HT-6P	$2,117	3,262 lbs.	20,021
2102	1011	2d Sed-6P	$1,912	3,177 lbs.	205,545
2124	1011A	2d Cpe-6P	$1,971	3,182 lbs.	56,382
2154	1037	2d HT-6P	$2,063	3,204 lbs.	18,616
2129	1063F	2d Sta Wag-6P	$2,215	3,344 lbs.	22,038
2109	1062F	4d Sta Wag-6P	$2,263	3,381 lbs.	113,656
2119	1062FC	4d Sta Wag-9P	$2,348	3,500 lbs.	17,988
TWO-TEN SERIES V-8					
2103	1019	4d Sed-6P	$2,054	3,192 lbs.	—
2113	1039	4d HT-6P	$2,216	3,242 lbs.	—
2102	1011	2d Sed-6P	$2,011	3,157 lbs.	—
2124	1011A	2d Cpe-6P	$2,070	3,162 lbs.	—
2154	1037	2d HT-6P	$2,162	3,184 lbs.	—
2129	1063F	2d Sta Wag-6P	$2,314	3,324 lbs.	—
2109	1062F	4d Sta Wag-6P	$2,362	3,361 lbs.	—
2119	1062FC	4d Sta Wag-9P	$2,447	3,480 lbs.	—

NOTE: Production totals reflect combined six-cylinder and V-8 production for each body style.

BEL AIR—SERIES 2400 C: The luxurious Bel Air was richly appointed inside and out. Bel Air nameplates and emblems appeared on rear fenders. The slanting sash molding blended into a horizontal chrome belt that ran forward to the headlamp crease and doubled back, running horizontally to below the rear side windows and then, sweeping down towards the rear bumper ends. Chrome wheel covers were standard equipment. There was an extra chrome treatment around and between all window groups. Three-spoke steering wheels and deep-pile carpets graced all models except the Beauville nine-passenger station wagon which had vinyl coated rubber floor mats as standard equipment. Exclusive Bel Air models included a convertible and the two-door Nomad station wagon, the latter having a unique two-door hardtop roof treatment. All Bel Airs had electric clocks and lighted, lockable glove compartments. All 1956 Chevrolets with V-8 power had large, V-shaped emblems below the crest ornaments on the hood and deck.

BEL AIR SERIES 2400 C

BEL AIR SERIES SIX-CYL

Model No.	Body/Style No.	Body Type & Seating	Factory Price	Shipping Weight	Production Total
2403	1019D	4d Sed-6P	$2,068	3,231 lbs.	269,798
2413	1039D	4d HT-6P	$2,230	3,280 lbs.	103,602
2402	1011D	2d Sed-6P	$2,025	3,197 lbs.	104,849
2454	1037D	2d HT-6P	$2,176	3,232 lbs.	128,382
2434	1067D	2d Conv-SP	$2,344	3,340 lbs.	41,268
2429	1064DF	2d Nomad-6P	$2,608	3,362 lbs.	7,886
2419	1062DF	4d Sta Wag-9P	$2,482	3,516 lbs.	13,268

BEL AIR SERIES V-8

Model No.	Body/Style No.	Body Type & Seating	Factory Price	Shipping Weight	Production Total
2403	1019D	4d Sed-6P	$2,167	3,211 lbs.	—
2413	1039D	4d HT-6P	$2,329	3,260 lbs.	—
2402	1011D	2d Sed-6P	$2,124	3,177 lbs.	—
2454	1037D	2d HT-6P	$2,275	3,212 lbs.	—
2434	1067D	2d Conv-SP	$2,443	3,320 lbs.	—
2429	1064DF	2d Nomad-6P	$2,707	3,342 lbs.	—
2419	1062DF	4d Sta Wag-9P	$2,581	3,496 lbs.	—

NOTE: Production totals reflect combined six-cylinder and V-8 production for each body style.

CORVETTE SERIES—V-8—SERIES E2934: In 1956, the Corvette began to define itself as a true American sports car. A lot of people would have been perfectly content if Chevrolet had frozen Corvette styling with the 1956 model. The same basic grille styling was kept intact, but the grille teeth looked a bit slimmer. Chevrolet styling studio chief Clare MacKichan directed the 1956 redesign, which was somewhat inspired by the thrusting headlamps and twin-bulge hood of the Mercedes-Benz 300SL gullwing coupe. There were new front fenders with chrome-rimmed headlights; glass windows; external door handles; chrome-outlined concave side body coves and sloping, tail light-integrated rear fenders. The dash layout remained the same as in the past. The 1956 rear view mirror, located on the center of the top of the dash, was adjusted by using a thumbscrew. Improved-fit soft convertible tops were standard and a power top was optional, as was a removable fiberglass hardtop. Upholstery colors were limited to Beige or Red, but seven nitro-cellulose lacquer body colors were available. They were Onyx Black with a Silver panel (Black or White soft top); Polo

This 1956 Corvette features Arctic Blue paint. (Jerry Heasley)

White with a Silver panel (Black or White soft top); Venetian Red with a Beige panel (Beige or White soft top); Cascade Green with a Beige panel (Beige or White soft top); Aztec Copper with a Beige panel (Beige or White soft top); Arctic Blue with a Silver panel (Beige or White soft top) and Inca Silver with an Imperial Ivory panel (Black or White soft top).

CORVETTE

Model No.	Body/Style No.	Body Type & Seating	Factory Price	Shipping Weight	Production Total
2934	2934	2-dr Conv-2P	$2,900	2,730 lbs.	3,467

NOTE: *Powerglide adds 95 pounds to weight.*

ENGINES:

BASE SIX-CYLINDER: Overhead-valve. Cast-iron block. Displacement: 235.5 cid. Bore and stroke: 3 9/16 x 3 15/16 in. Compression ratio: 8.0:1. Brake hp: 140 at 4200 rpm. Four main bearings. Hydraulic valve lifters. Carburetor: (Powerglide) Rochester one-barrel Model 7007200 or Carter one-barrel Model 2101S, (standard shift) Rochester one-barrel Model 7007181. Cooling system capacity without heater: 16 qt. Crankcase capacity (less filter): 5 qt. Engine codes: Z, ZC or Y.

TURBO-FIRE BASE V-8 (MANUAL TRANSMISSION): Overhead-valve. Cast-iron block and head. Bore and stroke: 3.75 x 3.00 in. Displacement: 265 cid. Compression ratio: 8.0:1. Brake hp: 162 at 4400 rpm. Taxable hp: 45. Torque: 257 lbs.-ft. at 2200. Five main bearings. Hydraulic valve lifters. Crankcase capacity: 4 qt. (add 1 qt. for new filter). Cooling system capacity: 16 qt. (add 1 qt. for heater). Carburetor: Rochester 2BC two-barrel. Engine codes: G, GC, GQ, GF, GJ and GK.

TURBO-FIRE BASE V-8 (POWERGLIDE TRANSMISSION): Overhead-valve. Cast-iron block and head. Bore and stroke: 3.75 x 3.00 in. Displacement: 265 cid. Compression ratio: 8.0:1. Brake hp: 170 at 4400 rpm. Taxable hp: 45. Torque: 257 lbs.-ft. at 2400. Five main bearings. Hydraulic valve lifters. Crankcase capacity: 4 qt. (add 1 qt. for new filter). Cooling system capacity: 16 qt. (add 1 qt. for heater). Carburetor: Rochester 2BC or Carter 2286-S two-barrel. Engine code: GL, F, FC or FD.

TURBO-FIRE 205 OPTIONAL V-8: Overhead-valve. Cast-iron block and head. Bore and stroke: 3.75 x 3.00 in. Displacement: 265 cid. Compression ratio: 9.25:1. Brake hp: 205 at 4600 rpm. Taxable hp: 45.0. Torque: 268 lbs.-ft. at 3000. Five main bearings. Hydraulic valve lifters. Crankcase capacity: 4 qt. (add 1 qt. for new filter). Cooling system capacity: 16 qt. (add 1 qt. for heater). Carburetor: Rochester 4 BC four-barrel. Dual exhausts. Engine code: GE, GM, GN or FB.

TURBO-FIRE 225 OPTIONAL V-8: Overhead-valve. Cast-iron block and head. Bore and stroke: 3.75 x 3.00 in. Displacement: 265 cid. Compression ratio: 9.25:1. Brake hp: 225 at 5200 rpm. Taxable hp: 45. Torque: 270 lbs.-ft. at 3600. Five main bearings. Solid valve lifters. Crankcase capacity: 4 qt. (add 1 qt. for new filter). Cooling system capacity: 16 qt. (add 1 qt. for heater). Carburetors: Dual Carter four-barrel. Dual exhausts. Engine: GR and FG.

CHASSIS: Wheelbase: 115 in. Overall length: (station wagons) 200.8 in., (all other models) 197.5 in. Front tread: 58 in. Rear tread: 58.9 in. Tires: (station wagons) 6.70 x 15 six-ply on nine-passenger models, (all other models) 6.70 x 15 four-ply, (optional) 7.10 x 15 four-ply. Fuel tank capacity: 16 gal. 12-volt electrical system. **Corvette chassis:** Wheelbase: 102 inches. Overall length: 167 inches. Front tread: 57 inches. Rear tread: 58.8 inches. Tires: 6.70 x 15. Frame: Welded steel box-section type. Front suspension: Coil springs, tube shocks and stabilizer bar. Rear suspension: Leaf springs, tube shocks and solid rear axle. Drum brakes. Steel disk wheels. Axle ratio: 3.55:1

OPTIONS: Power steering ($92). Power brakes ($38). Accelerator cover. Oil bath air cleaner. Air conditioner (V-8 only). Armrests for One-Fifty. Autronic Eye. Back-up lights. Chrome sill moldings. Park brake signal lamp. Power seat (except One-Fifty). Lighted cigarette lighter. Electric clock (except Bel Air). Eleven-in. diameter, heavy-duty clutch. Optional colors (paint or convertible top). Compass. Courtesy lights. Custom color interior. Door edge guards. Door handle shields. Exhaust extension. Fender guards. Fender top moldings. Floor mats. Locking gas cap. Heavy-duty generators. Deluxe heater and defroster. Recirculating heater and defroster. Tinted glass. Glove box lamp as option. Six-cylinder governor. Vibrator horn. License frames. Power convertible top. Vanity mirror. Oil filter. Chrome grille guard. Insect screen. Radio antennas. Radio (manual, push-button or signal-seeking). Rear speaker. Rain deflectors. Rearview mirrors (three types). Seat covers. Ventilated seat pad. Electric shaver. Spotlights. Heavy-duty springs. Right-hand sun visor for One-Fifty. Whitewall and oversize tires. Tissue dispenser. Tool kit. Traffic light viewer. Trunk light. Under-hood light. Continental wheel carrier. Wheel covers. Wire wheel covers. Power windows (except One-Fifty). Plastic windshield glare shield. Outside sun visor. Windshield washers (automatic or foot operated). De-icing wiper blades. Dual electric wipers. Wiring junction block. Three-speed manual transmission with column-mounted control was standard. Overdrive was available on the manual transmission at $108 extra. Powerglide two-speed automatic transmission was available at $189 extra.

HISTORICAL FOOTNOTES: Dealer introductions were held in November 1955. Model-year production equaled 1,574,740 units. Calendar-year sales hit 1,621,004. Chevrolet was America's number one automaker. The Two-Ten club coupe was called the Del Ray coupe. The One-Fifty utility coupe was the equivalent of the traditional business coupe and had a single front bench seat with raised storage compartment platform behind. All four-door hardtops were called sport sedans, two-door hardtops were called Sport coupes. Nine-passenger station wagons were called Beauvilles. Four-door conventional station wagons were called Townsman wagons. Two-door conventional station wagons were called Handyman wagons. The two-door Nomad station wagon had a slanting pillar roofline, a cross-ribbed roof and a slanting tailgate with seven chrome slat moldings. An innovation on all 1956 Chevrolets was that the left-hand tail light functioned as the fuel filler door. Chevrolet V-8s were actually lighter than sixes. The resulting power-to-weight ratio is one reason 1956 Chevrolet V-8s were named the "Hot Ones." Chevrolet general manager Ed Cole and Corvette chief engineer Zora Arkus-Duntov decided it was time for the Corvette to go racing in 1956. Zora drove one car to a two-way average of 150.583 mph at Daytona's Flying Mile. John Fitch also set a record of 90.932 mph for the standing-start mile at Daytona and 145.543 mph in the production sports car class. In the spring of 1956, at Pebble Beach, Calif., dentist Dr. Dick Thompson finished second overall and first in class in a sports car road race. Thompson went on to take the Sports Car Club of America (SCCA) 1956 championship with his Corvette. A 225-hp 1956 Corvette could go from 0-to-60 mph in 7.3 seconds; from 0-to-100 mph in 20.7 seconds.

The 1956 announcement day at Ferman Chevrolet in Tampa, Florida. (Ferman Chevrolet collection)

It's not always fun being a middle child. The '56 Chevy's "older sister" had the biggest débutante ball the auto industry had ever seen. The younger sister, while not as popular when young, grew to have fanatical following of suitors.

The 1955 Chevy was a tough act to follow. Chevrolet followed the act well with the 1956 models. The 1956 sales totals fell back down to 1954 levels, which was fine because 1954 had been a good year for Chevrolet as well.

There are lots of reasons to pay attention to the '56 Chevy. The '55 had a boxy, unfinished look when seen in its base-model form. The '56 Chevy looked more finished, even in its least dressy version. The '56 grille was more integrated into the style of the car and the large parking lights appeared to be part of the car, rather than stuck on. The rear fenders seemed longer and larger tail lights altered the proportions of the rear of the car. The overall effect of the design updates made the rear end of

the '56 look larger from the rear than a '55.

When looking at the '55 and the '56 from the side, the subtle difference between the rectangular rear wheel opening on the '55 and the flowing rear wheel opening on the '56 makes a big difference. The '56 rear wheel opening took the car's direction of travel into consideration.

The 1955 two-toning on the dressy Bel Airs fit the car perfectly and the 1956 two-toning was even more creative. Chevrolet added a four-door hardtop to the Bel Air lineup and called it a Sports Sedan. Its roofline was lower and flatter than that of the ordinary four-door sedan. This small difference in proportion made the whole car look lower. With the windows rolled down, the '56 Bel Air Sports Sedan was sleekest, lowest-looking Chevrolet made up to that time.

The more expensive versions of most cars usually have the most interesting features found in the car line, but Chevrolet had a secret hidden in its middle-line 210 series—the Del-Ray interior. The Del-Ray option

A 1956 Chevrolet Bel Air convertible looking at home in the Arizona desert.

existed in 1954 and 1955, but it appears the special interior grew more popular in 1956.

Most Chevrolet interiors had a combination of cloth and leatherette. The Bel Air interior in particular had sparkly cloth upholstery, but the Del Ray interior was all leatherette with a black and white pattern. To some eyes, the leatherette interior may have looked more modern compared to cloth interiors that harked of the past, but others have said they bought them because they were easier to clean and more practical for the blue-collar guy driving to work with a coffee mug in his hand and driving home with his grubby work clothes on. With a few wipes of with a damp cloth, the Del Ray interior was clean, stain-free and ready for the weekend.

The '56 Chevy has a loyal following of enthusiasts. Many feel that their favorite "Classic Chevy" is caught between the '55, which caused such a sensation when introduced, and the '57, which has a cult-like following. The '56 Chevy successfully carried the '55 design theme to conclusion and many long-standing Chevrolet dealers reported that they were a lot happier with the design of the '56 than they were with the '57.

People joke about middle children, but like any middle child, the '56 Chevy has unique qualities and a place of its own in history.

These two 1956 Chevrolets give very different impressions. Above, the Bel Air four-door hardtop sports sedan on the right has a lower, flatter roofline than the 210 two-door sedan, and it gives the illusion that the four-door hardtop is a much lower car. The full-width deluxe bumper guard on the Bel Air adds to the feeling of low width.

The 1956 Chevrolet used the same dash as the 1955, but instead of the bright-metal appliqué being covered with hundreds of tiny bowties, the '56 appliqué was enhanced with sweeping black lines. This decked-out Bel Air has a V-8 engine and three-speed manual transmission.

CHAPTER 8

Some long-standing Chevrolet dealers remember being disappointed in the appearance of the 1957 Chevrolet because, at the time, Ford and Plymouth were both all-new cars, and Chevrolet's 1955 ultra-successful styling was suddenly old-fashioned. The '57 Chevrolet's lack of popularity when it was new may have quickly made it the official kids' car for an entire generation. The same Chevrolet dealers who report the '57 Chevrolet being a poor seller when new also report that it was the most popular used car they ever had when they came back as trade-ins.

1957

Introduction

Though its body was essentially the same one introduced in 1955, the '57 Chevrolet looked brighter, more modern and larger than the 1955 and 1956 models. A Chevrolet medallion was set into a center cavity within a new horizontal grille bar. Windsplit bulges ran along both sides of the flat hood panel. They were decorated in front with bombsight ornaments. The headlights were set into small grilles housed in square-looking fender openings. There were screens above the headlights that guided air through ducts into the passenger compartment.

The 1957 Chevrolet instrument cluster seems obtrusive after the two graceful V-shapes of 1955 and '56.

While the base One-Fifty models were trimmed much the same as in 1956, the Two-Ten models were upgraded with double body-side moldings on the rear quarters with contrasting paint between them. Bel Airs had an even richer look with silver anodized insert panels between the twin moldings, gold grille highlights and lots of extra bright trim, including gold front fender chevrons.

Chevrolet listed triple-locking door latches and "High-Volume Ventilation" as new selling features.

The fuel-injected 1957 Corvette reached the magical one-horsepower-per-cubic-inch high-performance bracket. The Corvette's continuous-flow fuel-injection system was a joint effort of Zora Arkus-Duntov, John Dolza and General Motor's Rochester Division. Only 1,040 of the 1957 Corvettes were fuel-injected. A 283 hp fuel-injection 1957 Corvette could go from 0 to 60 mph in 5.7 seconds and from 0 to 100 mph in 16.8 seconds. It had a top speed of 132 mph. Another important option was the competition suspension package RPO 684 which included heavy-duty springs, shocks and roll bars, 16.3:1 quick-ratio steering; a Positraction differential; special brake cooling equipment; and Cerametallic brake linings. Dick Thompson and Gaston Audrey won the 12-hour Sebring Race in Corvettes and Thompson took the SCCA B-production championship for the second year in a row.

I.D. NUMBERS: Serial numbers were stamped on a plate on the left front door hinge pillar. The first symbol in the serial number indicated the model and series: A=One-Fifty 1500 series six-cylinder, VA=One-Fifty 1500 series V-8, B=Two-Ten 2100 series six-cylinder, VB=Two-Ten 2100 series V-8, C=Bel Air 2400 series six-cylinder, VC=Bel Air 2400 series V-8, E=Corvette series 2394. The second and third symbols indicated the model year: 57=1957. The fourth symbol indicates the assembly plant as follows: (A) Atlanta, Georgia, (B) Baltimore, Maryland, (F) Flint, Michigan, (J) Janesville, Wisconsin, (K) Kansas City, Missouri, (L) Los Angeles, California, (N) Norwood, Ohio, (O) Oakland, California, (S) St. Louis, Missouri, (T) Tarrytown, New York and (W) Willow Run, Michigan. The last six symbols are the production sequence number in the specific factory. Serial numbers used were: 57-100001 to 314393 for sixes, 57-100001 to 314393 for V-8s. The Fisher Body number plate on the right-hand side of the cowl gives additional information such as the body style number (see second column in tables below), the body production sequence number, the trim (upholstery) number code and the paint number code.

PAINT COLORS: Monotone paint colors for 1957 were: No. 793 Onyx Black, No. 794 Imperial Ivory, No. 795 Larkspur Blue, No. 796 Harbor Blue, No. 797 Surf Green, No. 798 Highland Green, No. 799 Tropical Turquoise, No. 800 Colonial Cream, No. 801 Canyon Coral, No. 802 Matador Red, No. 803 Coronado Yellow, No. 804 Inca Silver, No. 805 Sierra Gold, No. 806 Adobe Beige, No. 821 Dusk Pearl, and No. 823 Laurel Green. Two-tone color combinations available in 1957 were: No. 807 India Ivory/Onyx Black, No. 808 Imperial Ivory/Inca Silver, No. 809 Harbor Blue/Larkspur Blue, No. 810 India Ivory/Larkspur Blue, No. 811 India Ivory/Tropical Turquoise, No. 812 Surf Green/Highland Green, No. 813 India Ivory/Surf Green, No. 814 India Ivory/Coronado Yellow, No. 815 Colonial Cream/Onyx Black, No. 816 Colonial Cream/India Ivory, No. 817 India Ivory/Canyon Coral, No. 818 Adobe Beige/Sierra Gold, No. 819 India Ivory/Matador Red, No. 820 Colonial Cream/Laurel Green, and No. 822 Dusk Pearl/Imperial Ivory.

ONE-FIFTY — SERIES 1500: New side moldings appeared, but varied for each series, looking a little richer as they moved up the scale. The One-Fifty models were the plainest. They had exclusive use

To compete with Plymouth, Chevrolet grafted sharp fins on an otherwise rounded car to make the 1955 body last one more year, but the design works well when accentuated with Bel Air trim.

of the 1955-'56-style sash molding below rear side windows, which intersected an approximately half-length, single horizontal molding. This strip of chrome ran from the front door region to the trailing edge of the tail fins much like the Bel Air trim from 1955. Chevrolet script was affixed to the upper side of the front fenders. The fins had only partial outline moldings near their rear tips, which dropped to the tail light housing. The grille insert was done in anodized aluminum finish. Interior trims were the most basic, although the Handyman station wagon had a two-tone look inside. Round horn buttons were used with standard steering wheels.

ONE-FIFTY SERIES 1500

ONE-FIFTY SERIES SIX-CYL

Model No.	Body/Style No.	Body Type & Seating	Factory Price	Shipping Weight	Production Total
1503	1219	4d Sed-6P	$2,048	3,241 lbs.	52,266
1502	1211	2d Sed-6P	$1,996	3,216 lbs.	70,774
1512	1211B	2d Utl Sed-3P	$1,885	3,168 lbs.	8,300
1529	1263F	2d Sta Wag-6P	$2,307	3,411 lbs.	14,740

ONE-FIFTY SERIES V-8

Model No.	Body/Style No.	Body Type & Seating	Factory Price	Shipping Weight	Production Total
1503	1219	4d Sed-6P	$2,148	3,232 lbs.	—
1502	1211	2d Sed-6P	$2,096	3,207 lbs.	—
1512	1211B	2d Utl Sed-3P	$1,985	3,159 lbs.	—
1529	1263F	2d Sta Wag-6P	$2,407	3,402 lbs.	—

NOTE: *Production totals reflect combined six-cylinder and V-8 production for each body style.*

The 1957 Chevrolet Bel Air sedan and Bel Air hardtop have different upholstery patterns, but they share some of the same themes. Designers continued hiding the gas cap under the driver's side tail light housing (far left).

(Craig Murphy)

The 1957 Chevrolet Bel Air two-door hardtop is one of the most sought-after cars in the collector hobby. (Craig Murphy)

While it wasn't the highest-selling body style when it was new, the 1957 Chevrolet two-door hardtop easily became the favorite style among enthusiasts. This wonderfully restored Bel Air shows off an interior that was quite nice for the money. (Craig Murphy)

TWO-TEN—SERIES 2100: Distinct side trim and a richer interior distinguished this line from the 150 series. The body rub moldings began just behind the headlight area and gently sloped to the rear bumper ends, although the sweep was most pronounced towards the rear half of the body. However, there was a second, upper molding that branched off just below (and behind) the body belt dip. This top molding just about paralleled the general contour of the fins and ran rearward, to hit the back edge of the fender. Inside the two moldings, near the taillight, a Chevrolet script was placed. In many cases, this "inside" area was painted a contrasting color as part of many optional two-tone finish schemes. Other trim features were the same as used on One-Fifty models. Three two-tone interior schemes with cloth and vinyl combinations were available at standard prices. Despite its kinship to the lowest-priced line, this year's 210 looked more Bel Air-like, especially when done up in optional two-tone exterior finish. As in 1956, all Chevrolets with V-8 power had large, V-shaped hood and deck lid ornaments, which were bright metal-finished on the lower series.

TWO-TEN SERIES 2100

TWO-TEN SERIES SIX-CYL

Model No.	Body/Style No.	Body Type & Seating	Factory Price	Shipping Weight	Production Total
2103	1019	4d Sed-6P	$2,174	3,275 lbs.	260,401
2113	1039	4d HT Spt Sed-6P	$2,270	3,325 lbs.	16,178
2102	1011	2d Sed-6P	$2,122	3,230 lbs.	162,090
2124	1011A	2d Del Ray Cpe-6P	$2,162	3,225 lbs.	25,664
2154	1037	2d HT Spt Cpe-6P	$2,204	3,265 lbs.	22,631
2109	1062F	4d Sta Wag-6P	$2,456	3,466 lbs.	27,803
2119	1062FC	4d Sta Wag-9P	$2,563	3,566 lbs.	21,083
2129	1063F	2d Sta Wag-6P	$2,402	3,411 lbs.	17,528

TWO-TEN SERIES V-8

Model No.	Body/Style No.	Body Type & Seating	Factory Price	Shipping Weight	Production Total
2103	1019	4d Sed-6P	$2,274	3,266 lbs.	—
2113	1039	4d HT Spt Sed-6P	$2,370	3,316 lbs.	—
2102	1011	2d Sed-6P	$2,222	3,221 lbs.	—
2124	1011A	2d Del Ray Cpe-6P	$2,262	3,216 lbs.	—
2154	1037	2d HT Spt Cpe-6P	$2,304	3,256 lbs.	—
2109	1062F	4d Sta Wag-6P	$2,556	3,457 lbs.	—
2119	1062FC	4d Sta Wag-9P	$2,663	3,557 lbs.	—
2129	1063F	2d Sta Wag-6P	$2,502	3,402 lbs.	—

NOTE: Production totals reflect combined six-cylinder and V-8 production for each body style.

Onyx Black was a popular color choice on the 1957 Corvettes.

(Jerry Heasley)

BEL AIR—SERIES 2400 C: Extra richness characterized the Bel Air line in all regards. Side trim was arranged as on 210s, except the area between the molding "branches" was filled with a silver-anodized aluminum beauty panel. Three gold chevrons marked the forward side of each front fender. Also done in gold were such things as the grille insert, V-8 ornaments (when used) and Bel Air beauty panel script. Rocker sills, roof and window outlines, and the entire edge of the fins were all trimmed with bright metal moldings. There were also traditional Chevrolet/Bel Air crests on the rear fenders, near the golden script. Distinctive two-tone interiors were another highlight. The Nomad station wagon had carryover features with new 1957 styling.

BEL AIR SERIES 2400 C

Model No.	Body/Style No.	Body Type & Seating	Factory Price	Shipping Weight	Production Total
BEL AIR SERIES SIX-CYL					
2403	1019D	4d Sed-6P	$2,290	3,281 lbs.	254,331
2413	1039D	4d HT Spt Sed-6P	$2,364	3,336 lbs.	137,672
2402	1011D	2d Sed-6P	$2,238	3,237 lbs.	62,751
2454	1037D	2d HT Spt Cpe-6P	$2,299	3,283 lbs.	166,426
2434	1067D	2d Conv-SP	$2,511	3,414 lbs.	47,562
2409	1062DFC	4d Sta Wag-6P	$2,580	3,465 lbs.	27,375
2429	1064DF	2d Nomad-6P	$2,757	3,470 lbs.	6,103
BEL AIR SERIES V-8					
2403	1019D	4d Sed-6P	$2,390	3,272 lbs.	—
2413	1039D	4d HT Spt Sed-6P	$2,464	3,304 lbs.	—
2402	1011D	2d Sed-6P	$2,338	3,228 lbs.	—
2454	1037D	2d HT Spt Cpe-6P	$2,399	3,274 lbs.	—
2434	1067D	2d Conv-SP	$2,611	3,405 lbs.	—
2409	1062DFC	4d Sta Wag-6P	$2,680	3,456 lbs.	—
2429	1064DF	2d Nomad-6P	$2,857	3,461 lbs.	—

NOTE: *Production totals reflect combined six-cylinder and V-8 production for each body style.*

CORVETTE—V-8—SERIES E2934: The 1957 Corvette looked the same as the previous year's model. The thumb-screw-adjusted rearview mirror of 1956 was replaced with a lock-nut type that required a wrench to adjust. The big news was the availability of a 283-cid 283-hp fuel-injected V-8. Among the standard features were: dual exhaust; all-vinyl bucket seats; three-spoke competition-style steering wheel; carpeting; outside rearview mirror; electric clock and tachometer. Corvettes were now available in seven colors: Code 704 Onyx Black (Black, White or Beige top); Code 718 Polo White (Black, White or Beige top); Code 709 Aztec Copper (White or Beige top); Code 713 Arctic Blue (Black, White or Beige top); Code 712 Cascade Green (Black, White or Beige top); Code 714 Venetian Red (Black, White or Beige top) or Code 804 Inca Silver (Black or White top). White, Silver, and Beige were optional color choices for the side cove.

CORVETTE

Model No.	Body/Style No.	Body Type & Seating	Factory Price	Shipping Weight	Production Total
2934	2934	2-dr Rds-2P	$3,176	2,730 lbs.	6,339

ENGINES:

BASE SIX-CYL: Overhead-valve. Cast-iron block. Displacement: 235.5 cid. Bore and stroke: 3 $^9/_{16}$ x 3 $^{15}/_{16}$ in. Compression ratio: 8.0:1. Brake hp: 140 at 4200 rpm. Four main bearings. Hydraulic valve lifters. Carburetor: (Powerglide) Rochester one-barrel Model 7007200 or Carter one-barrel Model 2101S, (standard shift) Rochester one-barrel Model 7007181. (The "Blue Flame" six came with synchromesh, overdrive or Powerglide attachment.) Cooling system capacity without heater: 16 qt. Crankcase capacity (less filter): 5 quarts. Engine codes: A, AD or B.

TURBO-FIRE 265 BASE V-8 (MANUAL TRANSMISSION OR TOUCHDOWN OVERDRIVE): Overhead-valve. Cast-iron block and head. Bore and stroke: 3.75 x 3.00 in. Displacement: 265 cid. Compression ratio: 8.0:1. Brake hp: 162 at 4400 rpm. Taxable hp: 45. Torque: 257 lbs.-ft. at 2200. Five main bearings. Hydraulic valve lifters. Crankcase capacity: 4 qt. (add 1 qt. for new filter). Cooling system capacity: 16 qt. (add 1 qt. for heater). Carburetor: Rochester 2 BC two-barrel. Engine code: C, CD or CE.

The three small indentations on the 1957 Chevrolet front fender have gold metal trims in them on the Bel Airs, silver metal trims on 210s, and are empty on 150s.

The 1957 Chevrolet 150 side trim was very reminiscent of the 1955 Bel Air side trim, meaning the bottom-of-the-line '57 looked like the top-of-the-line '55, and that may have contributed to the dealers' trepidation and the public's cool reception toward the '57 Chevrolet.

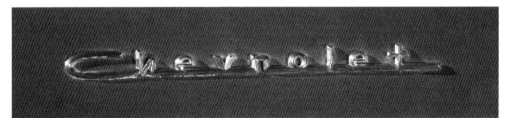

The simple Chevrolet script on the front fender of the 1957 model 150.

TURBO-FIRE 283 BASE V-8 (POWERGLIDE TRANSMISSION): Overhead-valve. Cast-iron block and head. Bore and stroke: 3.875 x 3.00 in. Displacement: 283 cid. Compression ratio: 8.50:1. Brake hp: 185 at 4600 rpm. Taxable hp: 48. Torque: 275 lbs.-ft. at 2400. Five main bearings. Hydraulic valve lifters. Crankcase capacity: 4 qt. (add 1 qt. for new filter). Cooling system capacity: 16 qt. (add 1 qt. for heater). Carburetor: Carter 2286-S or Rochester 2 BC two-barrel. Engine code: C, CD, CB, F, D, FA, G or E.

TURBO-FIRE 220 OPTIONAL V-8: Overhead-valve. Cast-iron block and head. Bore and stroke: 3.875 x 3.00 in. Displacement: 283 cid. Compression ratio: 9.50:1. Brake hp: 220 at 4800 rpm. Taxable hp: 48. Torque: 300 lbs.-ft. at 3000. Five main bearings. Hydraulic valve lifters. Crankcase capacity: 4 qt. (add 1 qt. for new filter). Cooling system capacity: 16 qt. (add 1 qt. for heater). Dual exhaust. Carburetor: Carter WCFB or Rochester 4 BC four-barrel.

TURBO-FIRE 245 OPTIONAL V-8: Overhead-valve. Cast-iron block and head. Bore and stroke: 3.875 x 3.00 in. Displacement: 283 cid. Compression ratio: 9.50:1. Brake hp: 245 at 5000 rpm. Taxable hp: 48. Torque: 300 at 3800. Five main bearings. Hydraulic valve lifters. Crankcase capacity: 4 qt. (add 1 qt. for new filter). Cooling system capacity: 16 qt. (add 1 qt. for heater). Dual exhaust. Carburetors: Dual Carter WCFB four-barrels. Engine code: EA, FD, GD, EH, CT, FG or DG.

There were no V's dressing up the front and back of the 1957 150.

RAM-JET FUEL-INJECTED OPTIONAL V-8: Overhead-valve. Cast-iron block and head. Bore and stroke: 3.875 x 3.00 in. Displacement: 283 cid. Compression ratio: 9.50:1. Brake hp: 250 at 5000 rpm. Taxable hp: 48. Torque: 305 at 3800. Five main bearings. Hydraulic valve lifters. Crankcase capacity: 4 qt. (add 1 qt. for new filter). Cooling system capacity: 16 qt. (add 1 qt. for heater). Dual exhaust. Induction system: Rochester fuel injection. Engine code: EJ, CH, FJ, DP, GF, EC, CY, EM, CR, FK or DH.

SUPER TURBO-FIRE OPTIONAL V-8: Overhead-valve. Cast-iron block and head. Special camshaft. Bore and stroke: 3.875 x 3.00 in. Displacement: 283 cid. Compression ratio: 9.50:1. Brake hp: 270 at 6000 rpm. Taxable hp: 48. Torque: 285 at 4200. Five main bearings. Hydraulic valve lifters. Crankcase capacity: 4 qt. (add 1 qt. for new filter). Cooling system capacity: 16 qt. (add 1 qt. for heater). Dual exhaust. Carburetors: Dual Carter WCFB four-barrels. Engine code: RB or EG.

SUPER RAM-JET FUEL-INJECTED OPTIONAL V-8: Overhead-valve. Cast-iron block and head. Bore and stroke: 3.875 x 3.00 in. Displacement: 283 cid. Compression ratio: 10.50:1. Brake hp: 283 at 6200 rpm. Taxable hp: 48. Torque: 290 at 4400. Five main bearings. Hydraulic valve lifters. Crankcase capacity: 4 qt. (add 1 qt. for new filter). Cooling system capacity: 16 qt. (add 1 qt. for heater). Dual exhaust. Induction system: Rochester fuel injection. Engine code: EK, CJ, CZ or EL.

NOTE: The famous Super Ram-Jet Fuel-Injection V-8 was one of the first to offer 1 hp per cubic inch.

CHASSIS: Wheelbase: 115 in. Overall length: 200 in. Front tread: 58 in. Rear tread: 58.8 in. Tires: 7.50 x 14 four-ply tubeless blackwall. Fuel tank capacity: 16-gal. 12-volt electrical system. **Corvette chassis:** Wheelbase: 102 inches. Overall length: 168 inches. Overall height: 51.9 inches. Overall width: 70.5 inches. Front tread: 57 inches. Rear tread: 59 inches. Tires: 6.70 x 15. Frame: Front suspension: Independent; unequal-length A-arms; coil springs, tube shocks. 15-inch steel bolt-on wheels. Standard rear axle ratio with three-speed 3.70:1; with Powerglide: 3.55:1. Optional axle ratios: 3.27:1, 4.11:1 and 4.56:1.

OPTIONS: Power brakes ($38). Power steering ($70). Overdrive ($108). Powerglide ($188). Turboglide ($231). Accelerator cover. Oil bath air cleaner. Air conditioner (V-8 only). Armrests for One-Fifty. Autronic Eye. Back-up lights. Chrome sill moldings. Park brake signal lamp. Power seat (except One-Fifty). Lighted cigarette lighter. Electric clock (except Bel Air). 11-in. diameter heavy-duty clutch. Optional colors (paint or convertible top). Compass. Courtesy lights. Custom Color interior. Door edge guards. Door handle shields. Exhaust extension. Fender guards. Fender top moldings. Floor mats. Locking gas cap. Heavy-duty generators. Deluxe heater and defroster. Recirculating heater and defroster. Tinted glass. Glove box lamp as option. Six-cylinder governor. Vibrator horn. License frames. Power convertible top. Vanity mirror. Oil filter. Chrome grille guard. Insect screen. Radio antennas. Radios (manual, push-button or signal-seeking). Rear speaker.

The 1957 Chevrolet Bel Air has a bright-metal appliqué across the dash, and the 150 has only a painted panel with a Chevrolet script.

Rain deflectors. Rearview mirrors (three-types). Seat covers. Ventilated seat pad. Electric shaver. Spotlights. Heavy-duty springs. Right-hand sun visor for One-Fifty. Whitewall and oversize tires. Tissue dispenser. Tool kit. Traffic light viewer. Trunk light. Under-hood light. Continental wheel carrier. Wheel covers. Wire wheel covers. Power windows (except One-Fifty). Plastic windshield glare shield. Outside sun visor. Windshield washers (automatic or foot operated). De-icing wiper blades. Dual electric wipers. Wiring junction block. The fuel-injection V-8 was priced $484 over the base price of a six. Safety seat belts and shoulder harnesses were new options this season.

POWER OPTIONS: According to the 1957 Chevrolet Passenger Car Shop Manual, six extra-cost power options were available in conventional (non-Corvette) models along with six gearbox selections. This provided a total of 17 optional engine/transmission combinations as follows:

POWER OPTIONS

CID	Comp. Ratio	Carb Barrels	Exhaust	HP @ rpm	Trans Combo	Valve Lifters
283	8.5	2V	1	185 @ 4600	3-4	H
SUPER TURBO-FIRE V-8						
283	9.5	4V	2	220 @ 4800	1-2-3-4	H
CORVETTE V-8						
283	9.5	2 x 4V	2	245 @ 5000	1-2-4-5-6	H
283	9.5	F.I.	2	250 @ 5000	1-4-5-6	H
283	9.5	2 x 4V	2	270 @ 6000	5	S
283	10.5	F.I.	2	283 @ 6200	5	S

NOTES: *F.I. — Fuel-injection. Transmission choices: (1) Three-speed manual, (2) Overdrive, (3) Regular Powerglide, (4) Turboglide, (5) Close-ratio three-speed and (6) Corvette-type Powerglide. H=hydraulic lifters. S=solid (mechanical) lifters. Corvette V-8s were not available in sedan deliveries. Lightweight valves were used only with SR high-performance camshaft and solid lifters. Some collectors maintain that a limited number of 1957 Chevrolet passenger cars came with four-speed manual transmission attachments, perhaps dealer-installed. This cannot be verified with normal factory literature. Cars with fuel injection engines wore special badges denoting this fact.*

HISTORICAL FOOTNOTES: Dealer introductions for 1957 Chevrolets were held in October 1956. Model-year production peaked at 1,515,177 cars. Calendar-year sales were counted at 1,522,536 units. Chevrolet outsold Ford by only 136 cars.

The beautifully new Bel Air Sport Sedan—one of 20 new Chevies. Sweet and low—and longer for '57!

'57 CHEVROLET!
SWEET, SMOOTH AND SASSY!

Chevy goes 'em all one better for '57 with a daring new departure in design (looks longer and lower, and it is!), exclusive new Triple-Turbine Turboglide automatic drive, a new V8 and a bumper crop of new ideas including fuel injection!

Chevy's new and Chevy shows it—from its daring new grille and stylish lower bonnet to the saucy new slant of its High-Fashion rear fenders. It's longer, too, and looks it.

And new style is just the start. There are new V8 power options that range up to 245* h.p. Then, you've a choice of *two* automatic drives as extra-cost options. There's an even finer Powerglide, and new Turboglide with Triple-Turbine take-off.

Go see the new car that goes 'em all one better. Your Chevrolet dealer's got it! . . . Chevrolet Division of General Motors, Detroit 2, Michigan.

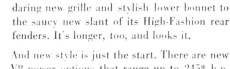

*A special 270-h.p. engine also available at extra cost. Also revolutionary Ramjet fuel injection engines with up to 283 h.p. in Corvette and passenger car models.

Chevy's new beauty wins going away! Body by Fisher, of course.

Venetian Red paint made the Corvette hard to miss. (Nicky Wright)

This car carried the most powerful Corvette engine available in 1957—the 283-cid/283-hp fuel-injected V-8. (Jerry Heasley)

The 1957 Chevrolet: Putting the "Cult" in Car Culture

The 1957 Chevrolet was a good car, but some long-standing Chevrolet dealers report being disappointed at the time in the appearance of the 1957s. Chevrolet fell to second place in the industry, which is still a highly respectable position, but it was a shock to Chevrolet and to the dealers who had enjoyed riding a record-setting wave of popularity in 1955.

When the 1957 Chevrolet was unloaded from the trucks, a chill went through the dealers because, right across the street, there were Ford and Plymouth dealers with cars that were all-new from the ground up. Ford's cars were bigger, longer, wider, and more in keeping with the times as the Jet Age moved toward the Space Age. Plymouth's slogan for 1957 was "Suddenly, it's 1960!" and Plymouth had, indeed, leapt years ahead of Ford and a decade ahead of Chevrolet with many mechanical advancements the other two didn't match. The Fords and Plymouths both had their problems, too, but they both made Chevrolets look small and narrow. Ford and Plymouth also offered a variety of V-8 engines, while Chevrolet still offered only one.

Still, the 1957 Chevrolet's virtues were many, and it was a good car. The 1955-'56 265-cubic-inch V-8 had evolved into the 283 with an integral oil filter, better engine oiling, and better reliability. Chevrolet still sold a high number of six-cylinder cars that cruised right along reliably and economically, and the sixes even had respectable acceleration for ordinary driving. Chevrolet enthusiasts report the 1957 V-8 model to be noticeably snappier on acceleration, and while the new Turboglide automatic transmission was troublesome, the good old Powerglide was a convenient, proven workhorse.

For ordinary driving, the Chevrolet was pleasant and roadable. While many car companies were hanging artificial air scoops on their cars to imitate the Jet Age, Chevrolets had real air intakes in the screens above the headlights, and these ducts took fresh air into the cabin and through the heater. Some say the ducts prevented rust above the headlights, which was common on many American cars at that time.

Decades later, without the 1957 Fords and Plymouths parked next to them, a '57 Bel Air hardtop with two-tone paint and all the trim makes for a very pretty car, but that's not what people always saw then they were new. Many people's first look at the '57 Chevrolet was when they saw a 150 or 210 sedan with either no side trim at all or side trim that resembled the '55 trim making an incongruous return on a car on which it didn't belong on. The '57 Chevrolet used smaller wheels than in 1956, and while the Bel Air's full wheel covers look great, the 150 or 210's small, dog-dish hubcaps accentuate the smaller wheels. In automobile design, proportion is everything, and in de-trimmed form, the '57 Chevrolet's proportions didn't work nearly as well as on the decked-out Bel Airs.

All American car companies' sales were affected by a minor recession in 1957 that grew into a serious recession by 1958. While some of Chevrolet's dropping sales in 1957 are attributable to the recession, a better economy might have been worse for Chevrolet because the car-buying public would have had more money and more choice, and they might have exercised that choice and chased after more expensive cars in addition to Ford and Plymouth.

As Mythology

Dealers consistently remember the public giving the 1957 Chevrolet a very cool reception, and some even had to take special precautions to show the car to their customers differently than they had with previous models. They also report the 1957 Chevrolet became the most popular used car they ever handled—much more popular as a used car than it had been as a new car.

The 1957 Chevrolet is held up as an American icon, representative of its era, and an expensive classic. The car that disappointed the dealers when new is the object of nostalgia so tightly focused and disproportionate that it overshadows the rest of the story—a story that's actually much more interesting than the myth.

High School Memories

Every man loves his first car. Much of the time, a young man's first car was a hand-me-down from mom and dad. The new owner and his friends would stand around the high school parking lot kicking tires and enjoying their newfound freedom. They thought of their worn-out, hand-me-down car as being *cool*. They would then declare their father's Olds, Buick, Cadillac, Chrysler, DeSoto or Nash *un-cool*—a dreaded "Dad's car" to be avoided at all costs under penalty of teenage humiliation.

Of course, the truth was that their parents had the good car. They were newer, more comfortable, more reliable and more technologically advanced than the kids' cars. Much of the time, a teenage boy would put a lot of money and work into building a hot rod that his mother's Oldsmobile would outrun at half-throttle.

The '57 Chevrolet was not popular with car-buying adults. As the recession eased, the public traded its '57s in. The '57 was the car the adults didn't want, so it quickly became the official kids' car.

The 1957 Chevrolet's one virtue over earlier kid's cars was that it was a pretty good machine for the money. It was small and light and could really go if equipped with a 283 V-8. This enhanced the '57 Chevrolet's image as a quick car. The '57 Chevy was the first car to so many people that it became associated with many happy times and nostalgia for pre-counter-culture American life.

The dashing new Corvette (left) and the Bel Air Sport Coupe.

Chevy puts the _purr_ in performance!

That new V8 in the '57 Chevrolet is as quiet as a contented cat and as smooth as cream. And it's cat-quick in response when you ask for action!

No household tabby sitting in a sunny window ever purred more softly than Chevy's new V8 engine. It's so kitten-quiet and cream-smooth that you can scarcely even tell when it's idling.

But when you nudge the accelerator, you know it's there, all right! It pours out the kind of velvety action that helps you be a surer, safer driver. Its right-now response keeps you out of highway emergencies. It over-powers steep hills with such ease they seem like level landscape.

New Chevrolet V8 engine options put up to 245* horsepower under your command. With 283 cubic inches of displacement, this beautifully designed V8 is a new, bigger and better edition of the engines that have put Chevrolet at the top of the performance ladder. It's sassy, sure—but as tame to your touch as a purring pussycat.

Try the smoothest V8 you ever put a toe to, and all the good things that go with it. It's available in any one of the bright new Chevrolet models you choose—all with Chevy's own special sweet and solid way of going. Stop by your Chevrolet dealer's . . . soon!

SEE YOUR AUTHORIZED CHEVROLET DEALER

CHEVROLET

1 USA
'57 CHEVROLET

*270-h.p. high-performance V8 also available at extra cost.

The 1957 Corvette retained the same body style as the '56. (Jerry Heasley)

Dealer Memories

Car dealers are always on the front lines for the good times and the bad. They sometimes know the cars better than the designers, and they sometimes see things the factory VPs of marketing never see.

Chevrolet handed its dealers a smash hit in 1955, and the 1956 Chevrolet was a beautiful continuation and completion of the '55. In only three years, though, the design was getting a little old when all-new cars from Chrysler showed up across the street, and times changed for Chevrolet dealers. Over and over, Chevrolet dealers relate the story of the 1957 Chevrolet's initial failings and eventual hit.

Holz Chevrolet had hosted a great party for the 1955 model, but in 1957, the experience was a little different.

"The nice thing about the 1959 and '60s models was that the customers either liked them or hated them," Jerry Holz recalls. "That was even more true for the '57 than the '59. It wasn't even close for second place in '55, but then, we got the '57s. Ford caught up to us with a brand new product that was more accepted that our Chevrolets. It just shows that people buy from appearances. At that time, Chevrolet was riding the crest of the 1955 models along with the nice '56s. The '57 didn't have the public appeal. What we had to do was sit the customer behind the wheel so they couldn't really see the outside of the car and couldn't see those semi-fins in the back and those two protrusions on the front. It's amazing today that the '57s are one of the hottest cars from the collector's standpoint. I will say the quality was quite high on the '57 Chevrolet. I remember going to

look at a new Plymouth in 1957, and when I was inside it, I could see light under the bottom of the door because the door didn't fit right."

Ron Mandeville and Lucille Mandeville-Benoit are brother and sister, and they grew up in the Chevrolet business. Their grandparents, Ephram and Donia Mandeville, founded Mandeville Chevrolet in the early-1920s in Manville, Rhode Island. Ephram died in 1929 from injuries he had carried since his service in World War I, and Donia continued to run the dealership. It's highly possible that Donia Mandeville was the first woman to be a full-fledged GM dealer with her name on the contract. Ron and Lucille run Mandeville Chevrolet in North Attleboro, Massachusetts, where the dealership moved in the early 1960s. They're too young to remember the 1957 announcement, but they enjoy passing along stories they heard from their grandmother and from their father, Fernand.

"I heard my father telling stories that the 1957 Chevrolet hardly sold brand new, although, it was one of the best-selling used cars in automotive history," Ron Mandeville relates. "To this day, it's one of the hottest-selling used cars there's ever been. The styling had gone a little too far past its mark, and its styling was radical enough that it made people go look at the '57 Fords instead. I think it all goes back to the rush to put fins on all the cars and clocks in all the dashes, and they came to market (with something that wasn't right for the time). My father spoke fondly of them because they sold so well as used cars, but he couldn't sell one new for love nor money. People were asking to buy his personal '56 Chevrolet after they saw the '57s. They had a lot of expectation of selling the '57 Chevrolets, and they didn't

This 1957 'Vette had the optional fuel-injected V-8. (Jerry Heasley)

sell. Chevrolet was shocked, but history being what it is, they came back as one of the best-selling used cars in Mandeville Chevrolet history."

Les Foss spent his entire career at Whitney's Chevrolet in Montesano, Washington. Foss had worked at Whitney's only a year or so when the 1957 Chevrolet appeared in the showroom, and he and his wife bought one. They sold it several years later, but they were able to buy it back in the 1990s.

"I don't remember the 1955 announcement as well as I remember 1957," Foss tells, "and what I remember about '57 was how disappointed all the Chevrolet dealers were because Ford was a brand new bigger, lower, wider car. Plymouth was even lower, longer, and wider. The '57 Chevy, on the other hand, was a warmed-over '55. The first Chevrolet Whitney's ever sold with air-conditioning was a '57 model. The man who ordered cars (for the dealership) thought he was ordering a deluxe heater, but he put the 'X' in the wrong box. I remember how unhappy

(the owner of the dealership) was when he returned from vacation and found the car had been ordered with air-conditioning. We made a demonstrator out of it, and we eventually sold it."

Foss says he still saw this air-conditioned Chevrolet running around the Olympia, Washington, area clear into the 1990s.

Jim Applegate is a longtime Chevrolet dealer in Flint, Michigan—a real GM town. Applegate's sales skyrocketed in 1955, but things cooled off quickly.

"We were spoiled because we expected a model change by '57," Applegate remembers. "Ford came out with a new car, and we had the old car, and Ford passed us that year. We expected the '55 success to keep going on. Of, course, '56 was pretty good, too. That's when (Chevrolet head) Ed Cole made up his mind we were getting a new car for '58. Then Plymouth came out with the Forward Look, but they were tinny cars with poor bodies on them."

the BEL AIR *sport sedan*

SHOWN IN IMPERIAL IVORY AND DUSK PEARL

Without vision-obstructing center pillars, this model captures all the joy of open-air motoring plus the all-weather comfort of a 4-door sedan. High set rear fenders reflect the daring sweep of Chevrolet's new lines. Even the wheels it rolls on are new!

the BEL AIR *sport coupe*

SHOWN IN INDIA IVORY AND CORONADO YELLOW

This adventurous hardtop has "new" written all over it—from bumper to bumper. The driver's view is new, too, with up to 75 square inches more glass area in the windshield, for safer viewing!

© 1956—CHEVROLET MOTOR DIVISION • GENERAL MOTORS CORPORATION

Applegate keeps a storyboard in his office showing the sales totals from several decades, and he tells the story through the numbers.

"In 1954, we sold 2,950 cars and trucks," he recalls. "In 1955, we sold 4,518. In 1956, we had dropped clear down to 2,521, and by 1957, we sold 2,384."

Applegate's numbers and the experiences of other dealers reflect the deepening economic recession of 1957, but they all maintain that the '57 itself played a part in the story. Dealers remember the '50s era and car culture fondly and their view of the '57 Chevrolet has changed to a nostalgic one.

CHAPTER 9

The Biscayne name was new for 1958. The Biscayne was the base-model Chevrolet, but it was still a pretty car and possibly the fanciest base-model Chevrolet ever made. (Dick Romm)

1958

Introduction

The 1958 Chevrolet had an all-new, one-year-only design. By adopting an all-new "Safety Girder" chassis, Chevrolet brought to market a completely re-engineered and restyled line. Body revisions included lower, wider, longer sheet metal, a new front end with dual headlights, gull-wing rear fender and deck sculpturing and revamped side trim treatments. New cone-shaped parking lights and tail lights were adopted. The '58 Chevy's increased width, length and glass area fit the times better. So did the luxurious Impala.

After a rather long process, four headlights became legal midway through the 1957 model run, but only Chrysler Corporation had been ready to make the change in 1957. General Motors went to the quad-headlight system in 1958, and it contributed greatly to the modernization of its looks and did, in fact, improve safety on country roads. (Dick Romm)

The styling bore a noticeable resemblance to "big sister" Cadillac, especially the Impala sport coupe roofline.

Selling features of the '58 Chevy included a "Glide-Ride" front suspension, "Ball-Race" steering, "Outrigger" rear springs, a "High-Volume" ventilation system, the use of "Triple-Locking" door latches and "Precision-Aimed" headlights. Chevrolet offered a "Level-Air" air-suspension for 1958, but it proved to be troublesome.

New names identified two series. Delray (now spelled as one word) was the base car line, followed by Biscayne and Bel Air. The Impala sport coupe and convertible constituted a top-of-the-line Bel Air sub-series. The models available within each line were altered, too. The sedan delivery was cataloged as a conventional model, but strangely not grouped with the station wagons. The wagons were now listed as a series unto themselves.

A new 348-cubic-inch Turbo-Thrust big-block V-8 competed better with Chevrolet's big-block-V-8 rivals. All '58 Chevy models with a V-8 engine had large, V-shaped ornaments on the hood and deck or tailgate.

The Corvette saw a lot of changes inside and out. There were now four horizontal headlights surrounded by chrome, and a pair of chrome spears in the back that have since become calling cards of the '58s, but weren't universally loved. The interiors were changed with instruments clustered in front of the driver, standard seatbelts and a few other tweaks. A variety of dual-quad and fuel-injected setups on the 283-equipped 'Vettes produced anywhere between 245 and 290 hp straight from the factory.

As usual, the four-door sedan was Chevrolet's most popular and comfortable body style in 1958. Even as a base-trim Biscayne, the sedan's shape rivaled its big sisters in the most expensive GM divisions in shape, trim, and two-tone styling.

(Dick Romm)

I.D. NUMBERS: Serial numbers were stamped on a plate on the left front door hinge pillar. The first symbol in the serial number indicated the model and series: A=Del Ray/Yeoman 1100 series six-cylinder, B=Del Ray/Yeoman 1200 series V-8, C=Biscayne/Brookwood 1500 series six-cylinder, D=Biscayne/Brookwood 1600 series V-8, E=Bel Air/Impala/Nomad 1700 series six-cylinder, F=Bel Air/Impala/Nomad 1800 series V-8. J=Corvette 800 series. The second and third symbols indicated the model year: 58=1958. The fourth symbol indicates the assembly plant as follows: (A) Atlanta, Georgia, (B) Baltimore, Maryland, (F) Flint, Michigan, (J) Janesville, Wisconsin, (K) Kansas City, Missouri, (L) Los Angeles, California, (N) Norwood, Ohio, (O) Oakland, California, (S) St. Louis, Missouri, (T) Tarrytown, New York, and (W) Willow Run, Michigan. The last six symbols are the production sequence number in the specific factory. The Fisher Body number plate on the right-hand side of the cowl gives additional information such as the body style number (see second column in tables below), the body production sequence number, the trim (upholstery) number code and the paint number code.

PAINT COLORS: Monotone paint colors for 1958 were: No. 900A Oynx Black, No. 903A Glen Green, No. 905A Forest Green, No. 910A Cashmere Blue, No. 912A Fathom Blue, No. 914A Tropic Turquoise, No. 916A Aegean Turquoise, No. 925A Colonial Cream, No. 930A Silver Blue, No. 938A Honey Beige, No. 923A Rio Red, No. 918A Anniversary Gold, No. 920A Sierra Gold, No. 932A Cay Coral, and No. 936A Snowcrest White. Two-tone color combinations were: No. 950 Onyx Black/Arctic White, No. 953 Arctic White/Glen Green, No. 955 Forest Green/Glen

Green, No. 960 Arctic White/Cashmere Blue, No. 962 Fathom Blue/Cashmere Blue, No. 963 Arctic White/Tropic Turquoise, No. 964 Aegean Turquoise/Arctic White, No. 966 Aegean Turquoise/Tropic Turquoise, No. 970 Arctic White/Sierra Gold, No. 973 Rio Red/Arctic White, No. 975 Colonial Cream/Arctic White, No. 980 Cay Coral/Arctic White, No. 982 Silver Blue/Snowcrest White and No. 986 Anniversary Gold/Honey Beige.

DELRAY—1100 SERIES (SIX-CYL)—1200 SERIES (V-8): Although the Delray models were the plainest Chevys, they still carried chrome body-side moldings. On the entry-level series, Delray nameplates marked the rear fender coves (indentations) of four body styles. These cars had single belt-line moldings and lacked bright metal side window trim. Delray interior appointments were the most basic types with standard steering wheels, rubber floor mats, and few bright highlights.

DELRAY SERIES

DEL RAY SERIES 1100 SIX-CYL

Model No.	Body/Style No.	Body Type & Seating	Factory Price	Shipping Weight	Production Total
PASSENGER CARS					
A	1249	4d Sed-6P	$2,155	3,439 lbs.	Note 1
A	1241	2d Sed-6P	$2,101	3,396 lbs.	Note 1
A	1221B	2d Utl Sed-3P	$2,013	3,351 lbs.	Note 1
A	1271	2d Sed DeL-1P	$2,123	3,529 lbs.	Note 1
STATION WAGONS					
A	1293	4d Sta Wag-6P	$2,467	3,740 lbs.	Note 1
A	1291	2d Sta Wag-6P	$2,413	3,693 lbs.	Note 1

DELRAY SERIES 1200 V-8

PASSENGER CARS					
B	1249	4d Sed-6P	$2,262	3,442 lbs.	Note 1
B	1241	2d Sed-6P	$2,208	3,399 lbs.	Note 1
B	1221B	2d Utl Sed-3P	$2,120	3,356 lbs.	Note 1
B	1271	2d Sed DeL-1P	$2,230	3,531 lbs.	Note 1
YEOMAN STATION WAGONS					
B	1293	4d Sta Wag-6P	$2,574	3,743 lbs.	Note 1
B	1291	2d Sta Wag-6P	$2,520	3,696 lbs.	Note 1

The dashboards in a 1958 Chevrolet Biscayne (above) and Impala convertible (below) are very similar, but the Impala has a much fancier steering wheel. (Dick Romm)

BISCAYNE—SERIES 1500 (SIX-CYL)—1600 SERIES (V-8): Only two body styles came under the Biscayne name, although, two Brookwood station wagons wore the same level trim. Since six-cylinder and V-8 models were considered separate series, the result was eight Biscaynes. The passenger-car styles wore Biscayne nameplates at the leading edge of the rear fender cove, but station wagons had Brookwood scripts in the same location. Biscayne side trim moldings outlined the upper and lower edges of the cove but did not connect. Ahead of the cove, a bi-level belt molding, with a slight forward taper, was seen. It was connected to the single, lower cove outline trim at the rear. Like the Del Ray models, Biscaynes came standard with small hubcaps, no sill moldings, no chevrons and no fender ornaments, but they did feature slightly up-market interior trims.

BISCAYNE SERIES

BISCAYNE SERIES 1500 SIX-CYL

Model No.	Body/Style No.	Body Type & Seating	Factory Price	Shipping Weight	Production Total
PASSENGER CARS					
C	1649	4d Sed-6P	$2,290	3,447 lbs.	Note 1
C	1641	2d Sed-6P	$2,236	3,404 lbs.	Note 1
BROOKWOOD STATION WAGONS					
C	1693	4d Sta Wag-6P	$2,571	3,748 lbs.	Note 1
C	1694	4d Sta Wag-9P	$2,678	3,837 lbs.	Note 1

BISCAYNE SERIES 1600 V-8

PASSENGER CARS					
D	1649	4d Sed-6P	$2,397	3,450 lbs.	Note 1
D	1641	2d Sed-6P	$2,343	3,407 lbs.	Note 1
BROOKWOOD STATION WAGONS					
D	1693	4d Sta Wag-6P	$2,678	3,751 lbs.	Note 1
D	1694	4d Sta Wag-9P	$2,785	3,839 lbs.	Note 1

The 1958 Biscayne four-door sedan.

Applegate Chevrolet gave away a new 1958 Chevrolet Bel Air to a lucky customer who had won a contest. Jim Applegate is on the left, and the winner was one of the men in the middle. (Jim Applegate collection)

BEL AIR—1700 SERIES (SIX-CYL)—1800 SERIES (V-8): Cars in the Bel Air series were enriched over other Chevrolets and were also endowed with two even more luxurious Impala models. The base Bel Airs had series name script and Chevrolet crests at the rear of the coves. The upper edge of the indentation was outlined with a single level molding that slashed down and back, below the body belt dip, to intersect an elaborate horizontal molding arrangement. This could best be described as spear-shaped moldings, with an indented concave contrast band towards the rear and a horizontally grooved, missile-shaped spear tip at the front. Also seen were four chevrons on the sides of the front fenders, four short vertical strips on the lower rear fender bulge, front fender top ornaments, chrome outlined side windows, grooved rear roof pillar beauty plates and full wheel discs. Interior appointments were rich and fancy. The Impala sport coupe and convertible were even more impressive. Trim features included Impala script, insignia and crossed-flag emblems at the front of the cove, broad, ribbed body sill panels, large dummy chrome-plated chrome air scoops ahead of the rear wheel wells, competition style two-spoke deep hub steering wheels with Impala medallions, Impala dashboard script, standard rear radio speaker grille with Impala script and medallion between rear seat back dip, and triple tail light arrangements. The Impala sport coupe had a chrome-edged, rear-facing dummy air scoop, and a curved contour crease molded into the back of the roof.

BEL AIR SERIES

BEL AIR SERIES 1700 SIX-CYL

Model No.	Body/Style No.	Body Type & Seating	Factory Price	Shipping Weight	Production Total
PASSENGER CARS					
E	1849	4d Sed-6P	$2,440	3,467 lbs.	Note 1
E	1839	4d HT Spt Sed-6P	$2,511	3,511 lbs.	Note 1
E	1841	2d Sed-6P	$2,386	3,424 lbs.	Note 1
E	1831	2d HT Spt Cpe-6P	$2,447	3,455 lbs.	Note 1
IMPALA					
E	1847	2d HT Spt Cpe-5P	$2,586	3,458 lbs.	Note 1
E	1867	2d HT Spt Conv-5P	$2,724	3,522 lbs.	Note 1
STATION WAGONS					
E	1893SD	4d Nomad-6P	$2,728	3,738 lbs.	Note 1

BEL AIR SERIES 1800 V-8

Model No.	Body/Style No.	Body Type & Seating	Factory Price	Shipping Weight	Production Total
PASSENGER CARS					
F	1849	4d Sed-6P	$2,547	3,470 lbs.	Note 1
F	1839	4d HT Spt Sed-6P	$2618	3,514 lbs.	Note 1
F	1841	2d Sed-6P	$2,493	3,427 lbs.	Note 1
F	1831	2d HT Spt Cpe-6P	$2,554	3,458 lbs.	Note 1
IMPALA					
F	1847	2d HT Spt Cpe-5P	$2,693	3,459 lbs.	Note 1
F	1867	2d HT Spt Conv-5P	$2,841	3,523 lbs.	Note 1
STATION WAGONS					
F	1893SD	4d Nomad-6P	$2,835	3,771 lbs.	Note 1

NOTE 1: Most Chevrolet production totals, after 1957, are available only in a form that indicates all series. There are no breakouts per series, model or engine type. For 1958, the totals were: four-door sedan — 491,441; two-door sedan — 256,182; four-door station wagon — 170,473; sport coupe — 142,592; sport sedan — 83,330; convertible — 55,989; and two-door station wagon — 16,590.

The Bel Air Sport Sedan—Body by Fisher, of course.

The Bel Air Sport Coupe—every window of every Chevrolet is Safety <u>Plate</u> Glass.

The Impala Convertible—supremely smart . . . superbly appointed.

Unmistakably modern in every lovely line — the Bel Air 2-Door Sedan.

Some people still buy high-priced cars,
but don't you wonder why?

No matter what you're willing to pay, you'll have a hard time finding any more car than this new Chevrolet wraps into one sweet, low-priced package. A relaxing ride, room to stretch out in, looks you can really be proud of—here's everything you'd expect in an expensive make. Plus the economy and dependability that have always been Chevy's specialty.

Your Chevrolet dealer will show you these and other things you'll be pleased with.

Slimline design—it's fresh, fine and fashionable.

Roomier Body by Fisher—sound, solid, stylish.

Sweeping new overhead curved windshield—and bigger windows—all of Safety *Plate* Glass.

Hi-Thrift 6—up to 10% more miles per gallon.

Vim-packed V8's—eight of them to choose from.

Full Coil suspension—further refined for a smoother, steadier ride on any kind of road.

Easy-Ratio steering—brings you reduced wheel-turning effort, new ease of handling.

Magic-Mirror finish—keeps its shine without waxing or polishing for up to three years.

New, bigger brakes—deeper drums, better cooled for safer stopping and up to 66% longer life.

Turboglide, Powerglide and air conditioning head a full list of extra-cost options.

Chevrolet Division of General Motors, Detroit 2, Mich.

The car that's wanted for all its worth!

1958 Corvette styling changes included dual headlights and hood louvers. (Nicky Wright)

CORVETTE—V-8—SERIES J800: Corvette styling was jazzed up for 1958. There were now four chrome-rimmed headlights with fender length chrome strips running between each pair of lights. As if that weren't enough glitter, fake louvers were placed on the hood. The grille was similar to the previous year, but had four fewer vertical bars. Three horizontal chrome strips were added to the new cove. A couple of vertical chrome bars decorated the trunk. They detracted from an otherwise graceful rear-end treatment. The wraparound front and rear bumpers were larger. The interior changed dramatically. The gauges were clustered together in front of the driver, rather than spread across the dash as before. A center console and passenger assist (sissy) bar were added. Seatbelts were made standard equipment. They had been a dealer-installed option in 1956 and 1957. There were six exterior body colors offered: Charcoal (Black or White soft top); Silver Blue (White or Beige soft top); Regal Turquoise (Black or White soft top); Signet Red (Black or White soft top); Panama Yellow (Black or White soft top) and Snowcrest White (Black, White, or Beige soft top).

CORVETTE

Model No.	Body/Style No.	Body Type & Seating	Factory Price	Shipping Weight	Production Total
J800	867	2-dr Conv-2P	$3,591	2,781 lbs.	9,168

ENGINES:

SIX-CYLINDER: Overhead-valve. Cast-iron block. Displacement: 235.5 cid. Bore and stroke: 3.56 x 3.94 in. Compression ratio: 8.25:1. Brake hp: 145 at 4200 rpm. Four main bearings. Hydraulic valve lifters. Carburetor: Rochester two-barrel Model 7012127. Cooling system capacity without heater: 16 qt. Crankcase capacity less filter: 5 qt. Engine codes: A, AE or B.

TURBO-FIRE 283 BASE V-8: Overhead-valve. Cast-iron block and head. Bore and stroke: 3.875 x 3.00 in. Displacement: 283 cid. Compression ratio: 8.50:1. Brake hp: 185 at 4600 rpm. Taxable hp: 48. Torque: 275 lbs.-ft. at 2400. Five main bearings. Hydraulic valve lifters. Crankcase capacity: 4 qt. (add 1 qt. for new filter). Cooling system capacity: 16 qt. (add 1 qt. for heater). Carburetor: Rochester 2 BC two-barrel. Engine code: C, CD, CB, F, D, FA, G or E.

SUPER TURBO-FIRE 283 OPTIONAL V-8: Overhead-valve. Cast-iron block and head. Bore and stroke: 3.875 x 3.00 in. Displacement: 283 cid. Compression ratio: 9.50:1. Brake hp: 230 at 4800 rpm. Taxable hp: 48.0. Torque: 300 lbs.-ft. at 3000. Five main bearings. Hydraulic valve lifters. Crankcase capacity: 4 qt. (add 1 qt. for new filter). Cooling system capacity: 16 qt. (add 1 qt. for heater). Dual exhaust. Carburetor: Carter WCFB or Rochester 4GC four-barrel. Engine codes: CM, DB, EB, CQ, CG, DM, EJ and DG.

SUPER TURBO-THRUST 348 OPTIONAL V-8: Overhead-valve. Cast-iron block and head. Bore and stroke: 4.125 x 3.25 in. Displacement: 348 cid. Compression ratio: 9.50:1. Brake hp: 250 at 4400 rpm. Taxable hp: 54.5. Torque: 355 lbs.-ft. at 2800. Five main bearings. Hydraulic valve lifters. Crankcase capacity: 4 qt. (add 1 qt. for new filter). Cooling system capacity: 22 qt. (add 1 qt. for heater). Dual exhaust. Carburetor: Carter WCFB four-barrel. Engine code: G or H.

283 FUEL-INJECTED OPTIONAL V-8: Overhead-valve. Cast-iron block and head. Bore and stroke: 3.875 x 3.00 in. Displacement: 283 cid. Compression ratio: 9.50:1. Brake hp: 250 at 5000 rpm. Taxable hp: 48.0. Torque: 305 lbs.-ft. at 3800. Five main bearings. Hydraulic valve lifters. Crankcase capacity: 4 qt. (add 1 qt. for new filter). Cooling system capacity: 16 qt. (add 1 qt. for heater). Dual exhaust. Induction system: Rochester fuel injection. Engine code: CR.

RAM-JET FUEL-INJECTED OPTIONAL V-8: Overhead-valve. Cast-iron block and head. Bore and stroke: 3.875 x 3.00 in. Displacement: 283 cid. Compression ratio: 9.50:1. Brake hp: 250 at 5000 rpm. Taxable hp: 48.0. Torque: 305 lbs.-ft. at 3800. Five main bearings. Hydraulic valve lifters. Crankcase capacity: 4 qt. (add 1 qt. for new filter). Cooling system capacity: 16 qt. (add 1 qt. for heater). Induction: Rochester fuel-injection. Engine code: EJ, CH, FJ, DP, GF, EC, CY, EM, CR, FK or DH.

The convertible was the lone Corvette body style in 1958.

The 348 big-block and the 283 small-block. The 348 was no quicker than the 283, but it was intended to be smooth and quiet, especially when hooked to the non-shifting Turboglide. The idea was to create a Chevrolet that drove like a Buick Limited.

(Dick Romm)

(Marc Mirabile)

SUPER TURBO-THRUST 348 OPTIONAL V-8: Overhead-valve. Cast-iron block and head. Bore and stroke: 4.125 x 3.25 in. Displacement: 348 cid. Compression ratio: 9.50:1. Brake hp: 280 at 4800 rpm. Taxable hp: 54.5. Torque: 355 lbs.-ft. at 3200. Five main bearings. Hydraulic valve lifters. Crankcase capacity: 4 qt. (add 1 qt. for new filter). Cooling system capacity: 22 qt. (add 1 qt. for heater). Dual exhaust. Carburetor: Three two-barrel. Engine code: FA, GB or HA.

SPECIAL SOLID LIFTER RAM-JET FUEL-INJECTED OPTIONAL V-8 (MANUAL TRANSMISSION): Overhead-valve. Cast-iron block and head. Bore and stroke: 3.875 x 3.00 in. Displacement: 283 cid. Compression ratio: 11.50:1. Brake hp: 290 at 6200 rpm. Taxable hp: 48. Torque: 290 lbs.-ft. at 4400. Five main bearings. Solid valve lifters. Crankcase capacity: 4 qt. (add 1 qt. for new filter). Cooling system capacity: 16 qt. (add 1 qt. for heater). Induction: Fuel-injection. Engine code: EK, CJ, CZ or CS.

SUPER TURBO-THRUST 348 OPTIONAL V-8: Overhead-valve. Cast-iron block and head. Bore and stroke: 4.125 x 3.25 in. Displacement: 348 cid. Compression ratio: 11.00:1. Brake hp: 300 at 5600 rpm. Taxable hp: 54.5. Torque: 350 lbs.-ft. at 3600. Five main bearings. Solid valve lifters. Crankcase capacity: 4 qt. (add 1 qt. for new filter). Cooling system capacity: 22 qt. (add 1 qt. for heater). Dual exhaust. Carburetor: Four-barrel. Engine code: FD.

SUPER TURBO-THRUST 348 OPTIONAL V-8: Overhead-valve. Cast-iron block and head. Bore and stroke: 4.125 x 3.25 in. Displacement: 348 cid. Compression ratio: 11.00:1. Brake hp: 315 at 5600 rpm. Taxable hp: 54.5. Torque: 356 lbs.-ft. at 3600. Five main bearings. Solid valve lifters. Crankcase capacity: 4 qt. (add 1 qt. for new filter). Cooling system capacity: 22 qt. (add 1 qt. for heater). Dual exhaust. Carburetor: Three two-barrel. Engine code: FB.

CHASSIS: Wheelbase: 117.5 in. Overall length: 209.1 in. Overall width: 77.7 in. Overall height: (Impala convertible) 56.5 in.; (Impala sport coupe) 56.4 in.; (other models) 57.4 in. Tires: (convertibles and station wagons) 8.00 x 14; (other models) 7.50 x 14. Full coil spring suspension; high-level ventilation; anti-dive braking and built-in leveling and foot-operated parking brakes were used this year. Fuel tank capacity: 20 gal.. 12-volt electric system. **Corvette chassis:** Wheelbase: 102 inches. Overall length: 177.2 inches. Overall height: 51.6 inches. Overall width: 72.8 inches. Front tread: 57 inches. Rear tread: 59 inches. Tires: 6.70 x 15. Frame: Front suspension: Independent; upper and lower A-arms, unequal-length wishbones, coil springs, anti-roll bar, tubular shocks. 15-inch steel bolt-on wheels. Standard rear axle ratio with three-speed 3.70:1; with Powerglide, 3.55:1. Optional axle ratios: 4.11:1 and 4.56:1.

OPTIONS: Four-barrel carburetor for 283-cid 230-hp V-8 ($27). Turbo-Thrust 250-hp V-8 ($59). Super Turbo-Thrust 280-hp V-8 ($70). Base fuel-injection 250-hp V-8 ($484). Powerglide transmission ($188). Turboglide transmission ($231). Overdrive ($108). Power steering ($70). Power brakes ($38). Power window control ($102). Front power seat ($43). Oil filter ($9). Oil bath air cleaner ($5). Dual exhaust as option ($16). Deluxe heater ($77). Recirculating heater ($49). Whitewall tires, size 7.50 x 14, four-ply ($32). E-Z-I tinted glass ($38). Electric wipers ($7). Safety panel padding ($16). Manual radio ($61); push-button radio ($84). Air conditioning ($468). Air suspension ($124). Two-tone paint ($32). Posi-traction rear axle with 3.36:1 or 3.55:1 ratio ($48). Other standard dealer installed accessories.

POWER OPTIONS
Optional engine and transmission combinations were as follows:

CID	Comp. Ratio	Carb Barrels	Exhaust	HP @ rpm	Trans Combo	Valve Lifters
SUPER TURBO-FIRE V-8						
283	9.5	4V	1	230 @ 4800	1-2-3-5	H
TURBO-THRUST V-8						
348	9.5	4V	2	250 @ 4400	1-4-5-6	H
SUPER TURBO-THRUST V-8						
348	9.5	3 x 2V	2	280 @ 4800	1-4-5	H
348 (M)	11.0	3 x 2V	2	315 @ 5600	1-5	S
RAM-JET FUEL INJECTION V-8						
283	9.5	F.I.	1	250 @ 5000	1-4-5-6	H

NOTES: (M) — Maximum performance V-8. F.I. — fuel injection. Transmission choices: (1) — three-speed manual; (2) — overdrive; (3) — two-speed Powerglide; (4) Turbo-glide; (5) — close-ratio three-speed; (6) — Corvette-type Powerglide; H=Hydraulic lifters; S=Solid lifters. (M) includes special performance-type camshaft and high-speed valve trains. Some of the transmission attachment data that has been interpolated as nominal factory literature is not specific about types of three-speed manual or automatic transmissions used.

HISTORICAL FOOTNOTES: Dealer introductions of 1958 Chevrolets took place in October 1957. The model-year total was 1,217,047 cars. Calendar-year production was 1,255,935 cars. The gas filler was now under a door in the trunk latch lid panel. On Impalas the center tail lights housed a back-up lamp. A great deal of bright metal trim on 1958 Chevrolets was made of aluminum. Almost 11 percent of 1958 Corvettes were powered by the 283-cid/290-hp fuel-injected V-8. A 1958 Corvette with the standard 230-hp V-8 and 4.11:1 rear axle could go from 0 to 60 mph in 9.2 seconds. It did the quarter-mile in 17.4 seconds at 83 mph and had a top speed of 103 mph. A 1958 Corvette with the optional 250-hp fuel-injected V-8 and 3.70:1 rear axle could go from 0 to 60 mph in 7.6 seconds and from 0 to 100 mph in 21.4 seconds. It did the quarter-mile in 15.7 seconds at 90 mph and had a top speed of 120 mph. A 1959 Corvette with the 290 hp fuel-injected engine took only 6.9 seconds to go from 0 to 60 mph and got slightly better gas mileage.

SWEET SEVENTEEN— AND NOT TO BE MISSED!

IMPALA CONVERTIBLE—another new luxury model in the Bel Air Series. How about those long, low lines! And *colors*— wait till you see the samples!

CORVETTE—America's only authentic sports car! Offers five spirited V8's, two with Fuel Injection;* three transmissions, including 4-speed manual shift.*

BEL AIR SPORT SEDAN—imagine getting this one with Turbo-Thrust V8* and Turboglide!* You'd have the smoothest power combination in Chevrolet's class.

NOMAD—star of a high-styled five-wagon lineup for '58! Seats for six in this one— and it surrounds you with luxury. Choose any Chevy engine; up to 280 h.p. in V8's.

BISCAYNE 4-DOOR SEDAN—in Chevrolet's middle priced series. Biscaynes, you'll notice, have a bright look of beauty that's all their own!

BISCAYNE 2-DOOR SEDAN—ready to take you for a super-smooth ride with Full Coil suspension at all 4 wheels! New air ride* is also offered.

BROOKWOOD 4-DOOR 9-PASSENGER —you can take half the neighborhood to school in this one! Upholstery is easy to keep clean; wears well, too.

DELRAY 2-DOOR SEDAN—you'll save with a Delray and still get everything Chevy's famous for: smooth ride, easy handling, real performance!

YEOMAN 4-DOOR 6-PASSENGER— comes with any one of Chevrolet's superb new engines. For biggest savings, choose the new 145-h.p. Blue-Flame 6.

YEOMAN 2-DOOR 6-PASSENGER— pile the family in and you're out for a good time; put in a cargo (up to a ½ ton of it) and you've got a willing worker!

*Optional at extra cost.

Here's Chevrolet's whole happy family. Here's styling that sets a new style—new developments in riding comfort that make the high-priced cars jealous—new peaks of performance (V8 or 6) in every model. Don't miss seeing and driving a '58 Chevrolet before you buy that new car. It's a beautiful way to be thrifty! . . . Chevrolet Division of General Motors, Detroit 2, Michigan.

NOTHING GOES WITH SPRINGTIME LIKE A BRIGHT NEW CHEVY! *Here are cars to rejoice in...sports-minded, fun-hearted and beautiful as all outdoors. The way they perform, ride and handle makes for the happiest driving you've ever known. Got spring fever? Trade it for that Chevrolet feeling!*

There's something about these new Chevies that was made to order for the warm, wonderful days ahead.

You can see it in the eagerness of their low-thrusting silhouettes. You can feel it in the spirited way they take to an open stretch of highway, in the nimble way they negotiate a winding country road.

These are cars to rejoice in—the surest, happiest cure ever invented for an old-fashioned case of spring fever. And the treatment starts with your first close-up look at the gull-wing glamor of that all-new Body by Fisher.

Every one of these new Chevrolet passenger cars is lower, wider and more luxurious in every detail. And every clean-etched line has a freshness you'll find on no other car in Chevy's field.

Once you're behind the wheel you'll find plenty of other exclusives that make driving more restful and zestful. Give some rein to the radically new Turbo-Thrust V8,* for instance, and see how it loves to shrink the miles out where they're long and lonesome. Or follow your wanderlust down a dipping backwoods road—and feel the putting-green smoothness of Chevrolet's new kind of ride.

Your local dealer will be glad to fill you in on all the details—including prices as low as Chevy's roofline!... Chevrolet Division of General Motors, Detroit 2, Michigan.

*Optional at extra cost.

*The dashing Corvette—
America's only authentic sports car.*

CHEVROLET

The Impala Sport Coupe—only Chevy's got this kind of gull-wing glamor!

YOUR PRIDE WILL PERK UP *whenever you're seen in your '58 CHEVROLET. One look at those low, wind-whisked lines and you know you're bound to be noticed. And you'll find still more to be proud of in the quick, sure way Chevy responds to your touch.*

Sure as it's a Chevy, you're going to be looked at when you drive this good-looker. Don't be surprised if you even hear a soft whistle of approval now and then. There's just something about Chevy's low, straining-at-the-bit beauty that makes people sit up and take notice.

The way this Chevrolet *moves* is something to be admired, too. Its quick-sprinting power, for example, and the reassuring way it keeps its poise, even on sudden dips and curves.

Another big reason you'll be prouder of a Chevy is that it's the only honest-to-goodness *new* car in the low-price field. There's a new X-built Safety-Girder frame . . . new Turbo-Thrust V8* . . . new longer, lower Body by Fisher . . . a choice of new standard Full Coil suspension or a real air ride.* Cars just don't come any newer—or nicer—than this one.

Make it a point to stop by your Chevrolet dealer's real soon. What he's selling is high on pride but low on price. . . . Chevrolet Division of General Motors, Detroit 2, Michigan.

Optional at extra cost.

Long, Low Luxury for 1958

The 1958 Chevrolet Impala was Chevrolet's first complete effort into the luxury field. It could be had with the 348 big-block V-8, the Turboglide automatic transmission, which was related to the Buick Flight Pitch Dynaflow, and the Level-Air pneumatic suspension. (Marc Mirabile)

The 1958 Chevrolets were good cars. The bodies was deliberately large for the first time since Chevrolet's days as a luxury make between 1912 and 1919, and dealers were generally happier with the 1958 Chevrolet than they had been with the 1957 models. The '58 was wider, longer and more comfortable, and it competed more directly with Ford and Plymouth, both of which had jumped way ahead of Chevrolet's styling in 1957. Even in low-priced Delray and Biscayne trim, the new

Chevrolet was more car for the money than the previous year, but Chevrolet reached high into the luxury world in 1958 with models, trim and mechanical options. Some of it worked, and some of it did not.

Impala

General Motors was so dominant by the late-1950s that the federal government was watching for violations of the antitrust laws. In many cities, a GM dealer's greatest competition did not come from Ford and Chrysler but, rather, from other GM dealers. Some say GM encouraged competition between its own divisions—Pontiac, Oldsmobile, and Buick.

Chevrolet joined the fight in 1958 and came out swinging with the Impala—a big, quiet, insulated car that looked more like a Buick than a Chevrolet. The Impala lived as a part of the Bel Air series and was available only as a two-door hardtop and convertible in 1958, and it distinguished itself with the Bel Air's chevrons on the sides of the front fenders and the Bel Air's spears on the fender tops. The Impala looked more massive because of a huge chrome scoop on the quarter panels behind the doors, wide bright-metal rocker panels, and a set of crossed flags below the roof pillar. The Impala two-door hardtop had special roof pillar trim and a rear-facing dummy air scoop on its roof. The two-door and four-door hardtops in the Bel Air line shared a roofline with Cadillac, and Chevrolet looked more like a luxury car than ever before.

With a 283 and a Powerglide, the Bel Air and Impala were adequate performers and had plenty of zip for the new freeways that were crossing the United States in a hurry. A new 348-cid "big-block" V-8 and the Turboglide transmission introduced in mid-'57 were also available to up the performance of '58 Chevys, although these options did not prove as durable as the 283/Powerglide combination.

Turboglide

From 1950 through 1952, Chevrolet's non-shifting Powerglide was a smaller version of the Buick Dynaflow, but the resemblance ended in 1953 when Chevrolet added a valve body to the Powerglide, making it a fully-automatic, self-shifting transmission. The Turboglide was a $231 option compared to the Powerglide at $188.

In 1958, Buick introduced an extra-high-tech transmission called the Triple Turbine Flight Pitch Dynaflow, which was standard on the expensive Limited and Roadmaster and optional on lower priced Buicks as an upgrade from the Twin Turbine Dynaflow.

Diagrams of the Buick Flight Pitch Dynaflow and the Chevrolet Turboglide are remarkably similar, with the Turboglide being somewhat smaller. They both have an extra-thick torque converter with more sets of stator and turbine blades. The stator blade-angle variations are infinite and designed to deliver the power from the engine to the transmission gearbox through exactly the right turbine at exactly the right ratio for the load.

Les Foss spent his entire career at Whitney's Chevrolet in Montesano, Washington beginning in 1956, and while Whitney's did not handle many Turboglides, Foss remembers them well.

"Oh yeah, they called it the 'Troubleglide,'" Foss recalls. "They had a lot in common with the Flight Pitch Dynaflow. What GM told us at the time was that there were three turbines with stream of oil pointed at the first one upon acceleration. Then, as the car started moving, the oil flow went through the second one, and by the time the car approached cruising speed, the oil was flowing against the smaller one. That's why it was so smooth. The Turboglide got a bad name, even though it was incredibly smooth. People were accustomed to having the low-range feature, but the Turboglide had the 'Grade Retarder' that reversed the flow of oil to make the car slow down. We had to repair one was because a guy pulled it down into Grade Retard and slammed the gas to the floor to pass another car. I never heard of those kinds of problems with the Powerglides in the '50s. The Turboglide was kind of like the Vega and the GM diesel engine disaster later. They probably brought it to market before it was ready. As I recall, it was more trouble-free by the end of its run, but it was costly to build, and people weren't buying enough of them."

The Chevrolet Turboglide continued through 1961, and anecdotal evidence indicates the transmission got more reliable by the end of its run.

The '58 Impala with a 283, Powerglide, and ordinary suspension is a good car and quite beautiful, but if the luxury items had worked like they should have, the ultra-loaded Impala with all that equipment would have had the characteristics of a Buick Limited at a Chevrolet price. (Marc Mirabile)

Plymouth and Ford both had big-block engines in '57 and Chevrolet felt like they needed a bigger engine. The 348 was good, solid engine and I don't remember them having any problems. When they bored it out and made the 409 out of it, it really became a legend."

Chevy dealer Chap Morris Sr. noted that the 348 "was no quicker than the 283. The wind-up was really something on the 283 and the 348 didn't wind as quickly. The 348 developed a lot of power a low rpm and was something that would pull a trailer better." Morris addd that the 348 gave exceptionally bad gas mileage for its size and insisted that a small-block Chevrolet V-8 would outrun it.

The 348 big-block was not a quick-revving sprint-runner meant to win a drag race. The use of the 348 in the '58 Chevrolet bears more resemblance to how straight-eights had been used in Buicks and Chryslers in the 1930s and '40s. They were meant to be smooth, quiet and luxurious. They were meant to feel effortless, as through they were coasting even when they were accelerating. The 348 Chevrolets were caught between two poles: the people who wanted big engines in luxury cars and were not terribly concerned with fuel economy and the typical Chevrolet buyer who wanted fuel economy. Most likely, the 348's poor fuel economy was noticeable in a Chevrolet than it might have been in a Buick or Cadillac.

While the 348 was not a great performer in stock form, it did provide a platform for further modification. David Holt's father helped him buy a new car when

The 348: A Weight Lifter, Not a Sprinter

Regarding the new 348-cid Chevrolet V-8, Foss says, "The 348 was a great, strong engine, but the disadvantage was that it was a lot heavier than the 283. Even though I'm sure the 348 cars had stronger springs, they always felt nose-heavy. The 348 was originally intended to be a truck engine and it wasn't as lively (as a 283). It didn't wind up as quickly as the 283, but it was really nice if you were going to pull a trailer behind your station wagon.

The 1958 Chevrolet was the biggest Chevrolet made since the expensive Chevrolets built between 1912 and 1919. Dealers were much happier with the '58 Chevrolet than they had been with the '57, in part because of their size.

(Marc Mirabile)

he graduated from high school in Pampa, Texas. Holt picked out a copper-colored '58 Bel Air two-door hardtop with a 348 and a three-speed manual transmission.

"It was a fast car the day I bought it," Holt recalls. "It did have that reputation as being more of a truck engine, but it would run 130 to 135 mph legitimately, after some modifications. It had the reputation of being not as quick as a 283. I had a lot of friends who had '57 Chevrolets with 283s in them and it was always a point of contention as to which one would go quicker."

With smooth luxury as its aim, the Impala could have reached up even higher if one more option had worked out.

Level-Air Suspension

Level-Air suspension was another '58 Chevrolet feature that had that "rushed-to-market" feeling. The goal was to have the car literally riding on air. A little air pump that filled rubber bags replaced the conventional spring suspension. The car floated along on air instead of metal-on-metal springs. Unfortunately, this system also had "real world" problems.

Former dealer Chap Morris Sr. saw a presentation on Level-Air suspension at a Chevrolet dealer meeting in 1957.

"Chevrolet repeated the same sort of mistake [they had made with Knee Action back in the 1930s] when they introduced a pneumatic ride, which was true air suspension," Morris recalls. "In 1958, they called it

Level-Air, and it was styled after the air suspension used in big freight trucks, and it leveled the car automatically and gave a car the smoothest ride possible. However, there were product problems with it, and as it sat over night, the air would leak out of it. I went to a meeting, and I was so enthused with Level Air that I told all my friends this was the only thing to have—a real break-through—and my friends believed me and bought it. I sold one to a lady who worked the night shift at the telephone office, and every morning as I went to work, I'd see her car leaning to the left side. The next day it would be leaning on the right side, and the next day, it

The use of the 348 in the '58 Impala was more like the use of straight-eights in Buicks and Chryslers in the 1930s and '40s in which smooth, quiet power was the goal rather than quick acceleration. The 348 was meant to feel like it was coasting even while it was accelerating. (Marc Mirabile)

would be sagging in the front or the back. There were some guys who worked across the street who used to take little bets on which way the car would be leaning in the morning. We took the Level-Air off a lot of cars. The bellows would go bad. That was an embarrassing one." In the end, many of the cars that left the factory with Level-Air suspension were retrofitted with conventional spring-type suspensions and only a handful of Level-Air cars have survived.

While some of the '58 Chevrolet features were problematic, the thinking behind them was aimed at the future. Chevrolet wanted to give the Chevy big-car styling and big-car features. And such goals ultimately resulted in the powerful engines, smooth-shifting transmissions and excellent suspensions found in modern automobiles. If better technology had been available back in 1958, the all-new Chevy introduced that year would have given buyers a true luxury automobile at an economical Chevrolet price.

CHAPTER 10

The 1959 Chevys, this is the Impala, were longer, lower and wider than any of their predecessors. The fuel-injected 283-cid V-8 is a rare find on a 1958 Impala. Revamped grilles and headlight assemblies were part of a whole new look for the 1959 Chevys.

(Angelo Van Bogart)

1959

Introduction The 1959 Chevrolets looked lower, wider and longer than any previous Chevys. They had unique horizontal gull-wing fins and cat's-eye tail lights. All Chevrolets compound-curve windshields were inspired by GM's 1955 LaSalle II dream car. This contributed to a big increase in the amount of glass. The front of the hood had two long, "jet-plane" air intakes, one on either side of center. A Chevrolet crest sat in the space between them. The parking lights were housed in the outer points of the slots.

The Chevrolet station wagon was a great choice for the young family on a budget. The fins sit a bit oddly on wagons, but the design worked.

Chevrolet called its new look "Slimline Design." The new body was larger, roomier and more comfortable. The cars were also quieter and better insulated. Dealers found them easy to sell.

The 1959 Chevrolet came in three profiles: sedan or hardtop with a sloping roofline, station wagons and flat-roof Sports Sedan. The latter had a wraparound rear window with a lip of the roof hanging out over it.

Biscaynes had only front fender side moldings. The Bel Air series was now the mid-range line. These cars carried a full-length body-side molding with a painted insert. On top-of-the-line Impalas, the painted insert carried a crossed-flags emblem. New Safety-Master brakes featured air-cooled drums and 27 percent more bonded lining area. Also featured were a full-coil-spring suspension and acrylic lacquer exterior body finish. Engine choices were greatly expanded with 13 options up to 350 hp.

The 1959 Corvette was basically a cleaned-up 1958. The fake hood louvers and vertical chrome strips on the trunk were removed. Interior changes included redesigned bucket seats and door panels, a fiberglass package tray under the sissy bar and concave gauge lenses.

I.D. NUMBERS: Serial numbers were stamped on a plate on the left front door hinge pillar. The first symbol in the serial number indicated the model and series: A=Biscayne/Brookwood 1100 series six-cylinder, B=Biscayne/Brookwood 1200 series V-8, C=Bel Air/Parkwood/Kingswood 1500 series six-cylinder, D=Bel Air/Parkwood/Kingswood 1600 series V-8, E=Impala/Nomad 1700 series six-cylinder, F=Impala/Nomad 1800 series V-8, J=Corvette 800 series. The second and third symbols indicated the model year: 59=1959. The fourth symbol indicates the assembly plant as follows: (A) Atlanta, Georgia, (B) Baltimore, Maryland, (F) Flint, Michigan, (G) Pontiac, Michigan, (J) Janesville, Wisconsin, (K) Kansas City, Missouri, (L) Los Angeles, California, (N) Norwood, Ohio, (O) Oakland, California, (S) St. Louis, Missouri, (T) Tarrytown, New York, and (W) Willow Run, Michigan. The last six symbols are the production sequence number in the specific factory. The Fisher Body number plate on the right-hand side of the cowl gives additional information, such as the body style number (see second column in tables below), the body production sequence number, the trim (upholstery) number code and the paint number code.

PAINT COLORS: Monotone paint colors for 1959 were: No. 900A Tuxedo Black, No. 903A Aspen Green, No. 905A Highland Green, No. 910A Frost Blue, No. 912A Harbor Blue, No. 920A Gothic Gold, No. 923A Roman Red, No. 936A Snowcrest White, No. 914A Crown Sapphire, No. 825A Classic Cream, No. 938A, Satin Beige, No. 940A Grecian Gray, and No. 942A Cameo Coral. Two-tone color combinations were: No. 950 Tuxedo Black/Snowcrest White, No. 953 Highland Green/Snowcrest White, No. 962 Harbor Blue/Frost Blue, No. 963 Crown Sapphire/Snowcrest White, No. 970 Gothic Gold/Satin Beige, No. 973 Roman Red/Snowcrest White, No. 987 Frost Blue/Harbor Blue, No. 988 Grecian Gray/Snowcrest White, No. 989 Cameo Coral/Satin Beige, and No. 990 Classic Cream/Aspen Green.

BISCAYNE—SERIES 1100 (SIX-CYL)—1200 SERIES (V-8): Standard equipment on Biscaynes included rear foam cushions, electric wipers, and oil bath air cleaner for V-8s, and they had a thin side-spear that only went from the front fender to the middle of the front door. The '59 Biscayne was the fanciest looking base-model Chevrolet made up to that point.

BISCAYNE SERIES

BISCAYNE SERIES 1100 SIX-CYL

Model No.	Body/Style No.	Body Type & Seating	Factory Price	Shipping Weight	Production Total
PASSENGER CARS					
A	1219	4d Sed-6P	$2,301	3,605 lbs.	Note 1
A	1211	2d Sed-6P	$2,247	3,535 lbs.	Note 1
A	1221	2d Utl Sed-3P	$2,160	3,480 lbs.	Note 1
BROOKWOOD STATION WAGONS					
A	1235	4d Brkwd-6P	$2,638	3,965 lbs.	Note 1
A	1215	2d Brkwd-6P	$2,571	3,870 lbs.	Note 1

BISCAYNE SERIES 1200 V-8

Model No.	Body/Style No.	Body Type & Seating	Factory Price	Shipping Weight	Production Total
PASSENGER CARS					
B	1219	4d Sed-6P	$2,419	3,600 lbs.	Note 1
B	1211	2d Sed-6P	$2,365	3,530 lbs.	Note 1
B	1221	2d Utl Sed-3P	$2,278	3,490 lbs.	Note 1
BROOKWOOD STATION WAGONS					
B	1235	4d Brkwd-6P	$2,756	3,955 lbs.	Note 1
B	1215	2d Brkwd-6P	$2,689	3,860 lbs.	Note 1

BEL AIR—SERIES 1500 (SIX-CYL)—SERIES 1600 (V-8): Bel Airs had model script nameplates and crests on front fenders. While Biscayne side moldings ran from the headlights to center front doors, Bel Air moldings ran full length and had painted inserts. Another enrichment was front fender top ornaments. Kingswood and Parkwood station wagons had Bel Air trim, but their own model script on front fenders. Standard equipment was the same as Biscayne, plus Deluxe features, front foam seat cushions, Deluxe steering wheel and power tailgate on Kingswood.

The 1959 Corvettes didn't have a lot of obvious changes from the previous year. (Nicky Wright)

BEL AIR SERIES

BEL AIR SERIES 1500 SIX-CYL

Model No.	Body/Style No.	Body Type & Seating	Factory Price	Shipping Weight	Production Total
PASSENGER CARS					
C	1619	4d Sed-6P	$2,440	3,600 lbs.	Note 1
C	1639	4d HT Spt Sed-6P	$2,556	3,660 lbs.	Note 1
C	1611	2d Sed-6P	$2,386	3,515 lbs.	Note 1
PARKWOOD/KINGSWOOD STATION WAGONS					
C	1635	4d Pkwd-6P	$2,749	3,965 lbs.	Note 1
C	1645	4d Kgwd-9P	$2,852	4,020 lbs.	Note 1

BEL AIR SERIES 1600 V-8

Model No.	Body/Style No.	Body Type & Seating	Factory Price	Shipping Weight	Production Total
PASSENGER CARS					
D	1619	4d Sed-6P	$2,558	3,615 lbs.	Note 1
D	1639	4d HT Spt Sed-6P	$2,674	3,630 lbs.	Note 1
D	1611	2d Sed-6P	$2,504	3,510 lbs.	Note 1
PARKWOOD/KINGSWOOD STATION WAGONS					
D	1635	4d Pkwd-6P	$2,867	3,970 lbs.	Note 1
D	1645	4d Kgwd-9P	$2,970	4,015 lbs.	Note 1

IMPALA—SERIES 1700 (SIX-CYL)—SERIES 1700 (V-8): For the "upper-crust" Chevrolet, identification features included Impala nameplates and crossed racing flags emblems. Both identifiers were mounted inside the painted insert area of the full-length side trim moldings, below the rear side windows. The front fender-top ornaments also had rear extension strips. Bright metal trim marked the deck lid center crease and tail light lenses. Closed models had simulated Impala-style roof scoops. Nomads had Impala trim with different I.D. script. Standard equipment was the same as on Bel Airs, plus electric clock, dual sliding sun visors and aluminum trim.

IMPALA SERIES

IMPALA SERIES 1700 SIX-CYL

Model No.	Body/Style No.	Body Type & Seating	Factory Price	Shipping Weight	Production Total
PASSENGER CARS					
1719	1819	4d Sed-6P	$2,592	3,625 lbs.	Note 1
1739	1839	4d HT Spt Sed-6P	$2,664	3,665 lbs.	Note 1
1737	1837	2d HT Spt Cpe-6P	$2,599	3,570 lbs.	Note 1
1767	1867	2d Conv-5P	$2,849	3,660 lbs.	Note 1
NOMAD STATION WAGONS					
1735	1835	4d Nomad-6P	$2,891	3,980 lbs.	Note 1

IMPALA SERIES 1800 V-8

Model No.	Body/Style No.	Body Type & Seating	Factory Price	Shipping Weight	Production Total
PASSENGER CARS					
1719	1819	4d Sed-6P	$2,710	3,620 lbs.	Note 1
1739	1839	4d HT Spt Sed-6P	$2,782	3,670 lbs.	Note 1
1737	1837	2d HT Spt Cpe-6P	$2,717	3,580 lbs.	Note 1
1767	1867	2d Conv-5P	$2,967	3,650 lbs.	Note 1
NOMAD STATION WAGONS					
1735	1835	4d Nomad-6P	$3,009	3,975 lbs.	Note 1

NOTE 1: *Chevrolet production totals are now available by body style only. For 1959, the totals were: four-door sedan — 525,461; two-door sedan — 281,924; four-door station wagon — 188,623; sport sedan — 182,520; sport coupe — 164,901; convertible — 72,765 and two-door station wagon — 20,760. No breakouts by series, model, or body style are available.*

CORVETTE—V-8—SERIES J800: In addition to some minor exterior changes, the Corvette got a tachometer, outside rearview mirror, seat belts, dual exhaust and electric clock added to its list of standard features. Sunvisors became optional. New concave instrument lenses reduced reflections. The optional four-speed manual transmission had a T-shaped reverse-lockout shifter with a white plastic shifter knob. There were seven exterior body colors offered: Tuxedo Black (Black or White soft top); Classic Cream (Black or White soft top); Frost Blue (White or Blue soft top); Crown Sapphire (White or Turquoise soft top); Roman Red (Black or White soft top); Snowcrest White (Black, White, Tan or Blue soft top) and Inca Silver (Black or White soft top). Blue, Red, Turquoise, and (for the first time) Black interiors were available. The armrests and door handles were in a different position, the seats had a new shape and a shelf was added.

ENGINES:

BASE SIX-CYL: Overhead-valve. Cast-iron block. Displacement: 235.5 cid. Bore and stroke: 3 9/16 x 3 15/16 in. Compression ratio: 8.25:1. Brake hp: 135 at 4000 rpm. Four main bearings. Hydraulic valve lifters. Carburetor: Rochester two-barrel Model 7013003.

Like all '59 Chevies, this Impala Sport Coupe is new right down to its safer Tyrex cord tires.

FRESH, FINE AND FASHIONABLE !

Chevy's Slimline design says new in a way all its own. And beneath the beauty there's new engineering that goes down deep. When you drive this one, you'll wonder why anyone would want a car that costs more!

From the clean thrust of its grille to the jaunty flare of its rear deck, this '59 Chevrolet is shaped to the new American taste. And you'll find its beauty has a practical slant too—with more seating room, new areas of visibility in every direction and a new Magic-Mirror

acrylic lacquer finish that requires no waxing or polishing for up to three years.

Once you're on the road, you'll discover such deep-down engineering benefits as bigger, better cooled brakes for safer, surer stopping; new easy-ratio steering and

a wide choice of power—from vim-packed V8's to a new Hi-Thrift 6 that goes and goes on a gallon. Your dealer's waiting now to show you the car that can give your pride a big lift at a low price. . . . Chevrolet Division of General Motors, Detroit 2, Michigan.

'59 CHEVROLET

What America wants, America gets in a Chevy!

The Bel Air 2-Door Sedan—Fisher Body beauty and Safety Plate Glass all around.

Every Chevrolet has a special way of leading your kind of life. Here—the Biscayne 4-Door Sedan.

CHEVROLET

Maybe you can't please everybody, but this car comes mighty close

Isn't it nice that a car can be fine and beautiful and still practical and economical? It's never been managed quite the way Chevrolet manages it this year. Here's all the style, room, comfort and performance anyone could want—along with Chevrolet's own famous brand of economy, reliability and durability.

Your Chevrolet dealer will show you these and other things you'll be pleased with.

Slimline design—it's fresh, fine and fashionable.
Roomier Body by Fisher—sound, solid, stylish.
Sweeping new overhead curved windshield—and bigger windows—all of Safety *Plate* Glass.
Hi-Thrift 6—up to 10% more miles per gallon.
Vim-packed V8's—eight of them to choose from.
Full Coil suspension—further refined for a smoother, steadier ride on any kind of road.
Easy-Ratio steering—brings you reduced wheel-turning effort, new ease of handling.

Magic-Mirror finish—keeps its shine without waxing or polishing for up to three years.
New, bigger brakes—deeper drums, better cooled for safer stopping and up to 66% longer life.
Turboglide, Powerglide and Level Air suspension head a full list of extra-cost options.
Chevrolet Division of General Motors, Detroit 2, Mich.

The car that's wanted for all its worth!

The hood louvers were gone from the 1959 Corvettes.

(Jerry Heasley)

Roman Red was one of the bold color choices on the 1959 Corvette.

(Jerry Heasley)

BASE V-8: Overhead-valve. Cast-iron block and head. Bore and stroke: 3.875 x 3.00 in. Displacement: 283 cid. Compression ratio: 8.50:1. Brake hp: 185 at 4600 rpm. Taxable hp: 48. Torque: 275 lbs.-ft. at 2400. Five main bearings. Hydraulic valve lifters. Crankcase capacity: 4 qt. (add 1 qt. for new filter). Cooling system capacity: 18.5 qt. (add 1 qt. for heater). Carburetor: Rochester 2 BC two-barrel. Engine code C, CD, CQ or D.

SUPER TURBO-FIRE OPTIONAL V-8: Overhead-valve. Cast-iron block and head. Bore and stroke: 3.875 x 3.00 in. Displacement: 283 cid. Compression ratio: 9.50:1. Brake hp: 230 at 4800 rpm. Taxable hp: 48.0. Torque: 300 lbs.-ft. at 3000. Five main bearings. Hydraulic valve lifters. Crankcase capacity: 4 qt. (add 1 qt. for new filter). Cooling system capacity: 18.5 qt. (add 1 qt. for heater). Dual exhaust. Carburetor: Dual Carter WCFB four-barrels. Engine code: CT, CU or DJ.

TURBO-THRUST OPTIONAL V-8: Overhead-valve. Cast-iron block and head. Bore and stroke: 4.125 x 3.25 in. Displacement: 348 cid. Compression ratio: 9.50:1. Brake hp: 250 at 4400 rpm. Taxable hp: 54.5. Torque: 355 lbs.-ft. at 2800. Five main bearings. Hydraulic valve lifters. Crankcase capacity: 4 qt. (add 1 qt. for new filter). Cooling system capacity: 22 qt. (add 1 qt. for heater). Dual exhaust. Carburetor: Carter WCFB four-barrel. Engine code: F, G or H.

CORVETTE RAM-JET FUEL-INJECTED V-8: Overhead-valve. Cast-iron block and head. Bore and stroke: 3.875 x 3.00 in. Displacement: 283 cid. Compression ratio: 9.50:1. Brake hp: 250 at 5000 rpm. Taxable hp: 48. Torque: 305 lbs.-ft. at 3800. Five main bearings. Hydraulic valve lifters. Crankcase capacity: 4 qt. (add 1 qt. for new filter). Cooling system capacity: 18.5 qt. (add 1 qt. for heater). Dual exhaust. Induction system: Rochester fuel injection. Engine code: CR or DH.

SUPER TURBO-THRUST OPTIONAL V-8: Overhead-valve. Cast-iron block and head. Bore and stroke: 4.125 x 3.25 in. Displacement: 348 cid. Compression ratio: 9.50:1. Brake hp: 280 at 4800 rpm. Taxable hp: 54.5. Torque: 355 lbs.-ft. at 3200. Five main bearings. Hydraulic valve lifters. Crankcase capacity: 4 qt. (add 1 qt. for new filter). Cooling system capacity: 22 qt. (add 1 qt. for heater). Dual exhaust. Carburetor: Three Rochester two-barrel. Engine code: FA, GB or HA.

SPECIAL CORVETTE RAM-JET FUEL-INJECTED V-8: Overhead-valve. Cast-iron block and head. Bore and stroke: 3.875 x 3.00 in. Displacement: 283 cid. Compression ratio: 10.50:1. Brake hp: 290 at 6200 rpm. Taxable hp: 48. Five main bearings. Hydraulic valve lifters. Crankcase capacity: 4 qt. (add 1 qt. for new filter). Cooling system capacity: 18.5 qt. (add 1 qt. for heater). Dual exhaust. Induction system: Rochester fuel injection. Engine code: CS

SPECIAL TURBO-THRUST OPTIONAL V-8: Overhead-valve. Cast-iron block and head. Bore and stroke: 4.125 x 3.25 in. Displacement: 348 cid. Compression ratio: 11.00:1. Brake hp: 300 at 5600 rpm. Taxable hp: 54.5. Torque: 350 lbs.-ft. at 3200. Five main bearings. Solid valve lifters. Crankcase capacity: 4 qt. (add 1 qt. for new filter). Cooling system capacity: 22 qt. (add 1 qt. for heater). Dual exhaust. Carburetors: Carter AFB four-barrel. Engine code: FG.

SPECIAL TURBO-THRUST OPTIONAL V-8: Overhead-valve. Cast-iron block and head. Bore and stroke: 4.125 x 3.25 in. Displacement: 348 cid. Compression ratio: 11.00:1. Brake hp: 305 at 5600 rpm. Taxable hp: 54.5. Torque: 350 lbs.-ft. at 3600. Five main bearings. Solid valve lifters. Crankcase capacity: 4 qt. (add 1 qt. for new filter). Cooling system capacity: 21 qt. (add 1 qt. for heater). Dual exhaust. Carburetors: Carter AFB four-barrel. Engine code: GD.

SPECIAL SUPER TURBO-THRUST OPTIONAL V-8: Overhead-valve. Cast-iron block and head. Bore and stroke: 4.125 x 3.25 in. Displacement: 348 cid. Compression ratio: 11.00:1. Brake hp: 315 at 5600 rpm. Taxable hp: 54.5. Five main bearings. Solid valve lifters. Crankcase capacity: 4 qt. (add 1 qt. for new filter). Cooling system capacity: 22 qt. (add 1 qt. for heater). Dual exhaust. Carburetor: Three Rochester two-barrel. Engine code: FA.

SPECIAL TURBO-THRUST OPTIONAL V-8: Overhead-valve. Cast-iron block and head. Bore and stroke: 4.125 x 3.25 in. Displacement: 348 cid. Compression ratio: 11.25:1. Brake hp: 320 at 5600 rpm. Taxable hp: 54.5. Torque: 358 lbs.-ft. at 3600. Five main bearings. Solid valve lifters. Crankcase capacity: 4 qt. (add 1 qt. for new filter). Cooling system capacity: 22 qt. (add 1 qt. for heater). Dual exhaust. Carburetors: Carter AFB four-barrel. Engine code: FD.

SPECIAL SUPER TURBO-THRUST OPTIONAL V-8: Overhead-valve. Cast-iron block and head. Bore and stroke: 4.125 x 3.25 in. Displacement: 348 cid. Compression ratio: 11.25:1. Brake hp: 335 at 5800 rpm. Taxable hp: 54.5. Torque: 362 lbs.-ft. at 3600. Five main bearings. Solid valve lifters. Crankcase capacity: 4 qt. (add 1 qt. for new filter). Cooling system capacity: 22 qt. (add 1 qt. for heater). Dual exhaust. Carburetor: Three Rochester two-barrel; (front) 7013973; (center) 7013974; (rear) 7013975. Engine code: FB.

SPECIAL SUPER TURBO-THRUST OPTIONAL V-8: Overhead-valve. Cast-iron block and head. Bore and stroke: 4.125 x 3.25 in. Displacement: 348 cid. Compression ratio: 11.25:1. Brake hp: 350 at 6000 rpm. Taxable hp: 54.5. Torque: 364 lbs.-ft. at 3600. Five main bearings. Solid valve lifters. Crankcase capacity: 4 qt. (add 1 qt. for new filter). Cooling system capacity: 22 qt. (add 1 qt. for heater). Dual exhaust. Carburetor: Three Rochester two-barrel. Engine code: Unknown.

CHASSIS: Wheelbase: 119 in. Overall length: 210.9 in. Overall width: 79.9 in. Overall height: (hardtops) 54 in., (sedans) 56 in., (station wagons) 56.3 in. Tires: (convertible and station wagons) 8.00 x 14; (all other models) 7.50 x 14. Fuel tank capacity: 20 gal. 12-volt electrical system. Corvette chassis: Wheelbase: 102 inches. Overall length: 177.2 inches. Overall height: 51.6 inches. Overall width: 72.8 inches. Front tread: 57 inches. Rear tread: 59 inches. Tires: 6.70 x 15. Front suspension:

Independent; upper and lower A-arms, unequal-length wishbones; coil springs; anti-roll bar; tubular shocks. 15-inch steel bolt-on wheels. Standard rear axle ratio with three-speed 3.70:1; with Powerglide: 3.55:1. Optional axle ratios: 4.11:1 and 4.56:1.

OPTIONS: Powerglide transmission ($199). Turboglide transmission ($242). Overdrive ($108). Super Turbo-Fire V-8 ($147). Turbo-Thrust V-8 ($199). Super Turbo-Thrust V-8 ($269). Power steering ($75). Power brakes ($43). Power windows ($102). Power seat ($102). Oil filter ($9). Oil bath air cleaner ($5). Dual exhaust ($19). Deluxe heater ($80). Recirculating heater ($52). Whitewall 7.50 x 14 tires ($32). Whitewall 8.00 x 14 tires, for convertibles and station wagons ($35); other models ($51). E-Z-I tinted glass ($43). Windshield washer ($12). Padded dash ($18). Manual radio ($65). Push-button radio ($87). Air conditioner, including heater ($468). Air suspension ($135). Positraction with 3.36:1, 3.55:1 or 4.11:1 gears ($48). Two-tone paint, on Biscayne ($22); on Brookwood, Bel Air, Impala ($27); on Parkwood, Kingswood, Nomad ($32). Power tailgate window ($32). Deluxe steering wheel ($4). Close-ratio four-speed transmission ($188). Wheel discs ($16). Two-speed wipers and washers ($16). Shaded rear window ($22). Front air foam cushion ($8). Deluxe Group with sun visor; front armrest; fender ornaments and cigarette lighter ($16). Heavy-duty 35-amp generator ($8).

POWER OPTIONS
Optional engine and transmission combinations were:

CID	Comp. Ratio	Carb Barrels	Exhaust	HP @ rpm	Trans Combo	Valve Lifters
SUPER TURBO-FIRE V-8						
283	9.5	4V	1	230 @ 4800	1-2-3-4-5-6	H
RAM-JET FUEL INJECTION V-8						
283	9.5	F.I.	1	250 @ 5000	1-3-4-5-6-7	H
283	10.5	F.I.	1	290 @ 6200	1-5-7	H
TURBO-THRUST V-8						
348	9.5	4V	2	250 @ 4400	1-3-4-5-6-7	H
SUPER TURBO-THRUST V-8						
348	9.5	3x2V	2	280 @ 4800	1-3-4-5-6-7	H
SPECIAL TURBO-THRUST V-8						
348	11.0	4V	2	300 @ 5600	1-3-5-6-7	S
SPECIAL SUPER TURBO-THRUST V-8						
348	11.0	3x2V	2	315 @ 5600	1-5-7	S

NOTES: *F.I. = Fuel-injection. Transmission choices: (1) three-speed manual; (2) overdrive; (3) two-speed Powerglide; (4) Turboglide; (5) close-ratio three-speed; (6) Corvette-type Powerglide; (7) four-speed.*

HISTORICAL FOOTNOTES: Dealer introductions were held October 1958. The Del Ray name was dropped. Calendar-year sales were 1,528,592 units. Model-year production totaled 1,481,071 cars. Ford and Chevy ran neck and neck, but Chevrolet turned out more cars built to 1959 specifications. Magic-Mirror deep-luster acrylic lacquer was introduced, along with improved Safety-Master brakes. A 250-hp fuel-injected 1959 Corvette with the 3.70:1 rear axle could go from 0 to 60 mph in 7.8 seconds. It did the quarter-mile in 15.7 seconds at 90 mph and had a top speed of 120 mph. A 290-hp fuel-injected 1959 Corvette with the 4.11:1 rear axle could go from 0 to 60 mph in 6.8 seconds; from 0 to 100 mph in 15.5 seconds. It did the quarter mile in 14.9 seconds at 96 mph and had a top speed of 124 mph. *Road & Track* described the 1959 Corvette as "a pretty package with all the speed you need and then some."

Bel Air 4-Door Sedan *in Highland Green and Snowcrest White*—Slender door pillars give this roomy family favorite the open, airy look of a hardtop. Chevy for '59 is lower, yet this model has actually more head room. Doors open high and wide for easy entry.

Chevrolet for '59—all new all over again! Wider in body, and *functionally* so—surer on the road, roomier and more comfortable for you and your family. Lower, yet with more head room in some models, greater entrance room in *all* models, greater visibility area all around. Matching its comfort and convenience are magnificent mechanical advances—in handling, steering and braking. In economy and durability. In safety, too, as typified by tires of new super-tough Tyrex cord. Altogether a fresh and *original* car . . . beautiful to be sure, with Slimline design, and practical its whole length through!

Nomad 4-Door 6-Passenger Station Wagon *in Aspen Green*—This top-of-the-line wagon will compliment you in any company, whether you're in denims or dress-up best. As in all Chevy models, the going's mighty steady—thanks to a husky new rear stabilizer bar!

Impala Sport Coupe *in Tuxedo Black*—There's a new "open air" look about this luxurious hardtop, thanks to Chevy's slender, shortened roofline and new Vista-Panoramic windshield which curves smartly into the roof to help you see traffic signals and signs without straining. The rear window, too, is higher, wider, handsomer, larger in area by 74 per cent—and for good looking every Chevy has Safety *Plate* Glass all around!

Versatile's the word for this Nomad 4-Door. Body by Fisher, of course.

Handiest helper a family ever had...'59 CHEVY! All five '59 Chevrolet wagons are as beautifully at ease with a delicate bit of greenery as they are with a rough-and-tumble cargo of kids. You can stow a whole half-ton of gear in Chevy's roomy back end—or use it as sleeping space on overnight excursions. And you can pick your power to fit your needs from thirty engine-and-transmission teams, including a lively 6 with wonderfully saving ways. Ask your Chevrolet dealer to show you the Chevy that's poised and priced to fit your own personal plan for happy living.

CHEVROLET THE CAR THAT'S WANTED FOR ALL ITS WORTH • CHEVROLET DIVISION OF GENERAL MOTORS, DETROIT 2, MICHIGAN

1959 Chevrolet

Plymouth's slogan for 1957 was "Suddenly, it's 1960!" Chevrolet's slogan for 1957 could have been "Suddenly, it's 1955!" In 1959, the roles reversed, and Ford and Plymouth were both updating three-year-old designs while Chevrolet was all-new.

The top-of-the-line Impala name and appointments were now applied to more body styles, including the four-door sedan—always the best-selling body style for most brands of cars in the '50s. The '59 Chevrolet was designed to be a more luxurious car than ever—a car that sparkled like a Cadillac, performed like a Pontiac, cruised like an Oldsmobile and drove like a Buick.

The design of the '59 Chevy reflected total innovation. Never before in history had an American automaker marketed three totally different cars in three consecutive model years. The role that Chevrolet played in the "Big Three" sales race was also totally reversed. The Chevy was suddenly an "all-new" car, while its competitors—Ford and Plymouth—were updates of three-year-old designs.

Car dealers of the day had mixed reactions to the '59 Chevrolet. One dealer remembers driving a brand new '59 Chevrolet through the streets of New York City and having a number of people run alongside the car, on the sidewalk, asking him what it was. Other dealers say customers either loved or hated the '59 design, which made their job easier. Those who loved the new design bought the gull-wing Chevys without much convincing.

None of the '59 GM cars resembled other models of the earlier '50s. Round, fat-fendered styling was out by 1959. Chevrolet had one of GM's wildest looks that season. Chevy pricing had always appealed to younger, more open-minded buyers and now the styling seemed to be geared to the same type of person. The cars looked long, low, wide and modern.

Chevrolet's most striking and comment-generating feature was its horizontal "gull-wing" tail fins. From the rear, Plymouth's higher, thinner fins suddenly looked narrow and uptight. The Ford's round, tubular fins looked heavy. Design trends had once again reversed. Chevy's fins met in the middle of the deck and formed a graceful V that suggested the flight of a soaring bird. The cat's-eye tail lights fit the design well.

The 1959 Chevrolet was its most graceful from the side where the fins become part of the car's forward motion. The front was wide, glittery and—some say—a bit odd. Different parts of the front of the car look as if they were designed by different people. Straight-on from the front, the Chevrolet developed a stance that, in silhouette, would take Chevrolet through 1964.

The dashboard had a set of pods that fit the car. The pods were a bit obtrusive, but they sat in the dash better than the ill-fitting pod of 1957. The design also marked a contrast with the ultra-plain 1958 dash.

The 1959 Chevrolet was not pointing the way to the future or rehashing the past. It was a 1959 car that said "Now!"

And, so, it ended—the glittering '50s. The decade began with Chevrolet drive trains that dated to the '30s and ended with engines and transmissions that served American drivers clear into the 21st century. The '50s began on dirt roads and ended on freeways. The decade of optimism and futurism may have worn the public out a bit, though, and the uniform rectangularity of American cars through the 1960s and '70s may have been a deliberate rest from innovation and a desire for lasting sameness. The '59 Chevy was a good last hurrah of '50s-ness for GM. It was a car of its time—low, lean and loud and worthy of a standing ovation as the curtain closed on an exciting decade.

The Powerglide Challenge

In an acceleration test, a '51 six-cylinder/non-shifting Powerglide hit 45 mph (far background) in 20 seconds, and '53 six-cylinder/ shifting Powerglide (left) and '55 V-8/Powerglide Nomad (right) both hit 45 mph in about 25 seconds. The '51 cheated a little by being held in Low and being manually shifted into Drive at about 25 mph, but if it had started off in Drive, it probably would have equaled the other two. The '55 V-8, once broken-in and tuned-up, should have beat the other two, but in spite of the hype in 1955, the 265 was not as quick as the 283s and 327s that came later.

Hitting the Real-World Road with Three Versions of Powerglide

Test tracks, proving grounds,

Motor Trend, Car and Driver...

Yes, but this is the real world. A car is only new once, and a 50-year-old car brings a mixed bag of traits and experience. Identical old cars can be as different from each other as people from different backgrounds.

There's only one way to test a car for real, and that's in the real world. Tom McCahill's creative, adjective-laden drive reports from the 1950s and '60s are fascinating, informative, and highly entertaining, but how do the cars test decades later? Three Powerglide-equipped Chevrolets met on Route 66 in California's Cajon Pass to find out.

The Place

U.S. 66 had merged with U.S. 91 and U.S. 395 to climb over the pass between the San Gabriel and San Bernardino mountains on the paths of 19th-century wagon trails. The highway started out as a narrow, treacherous, two-lane road with tight curves and sheer drops, but it improved through the 1930s and '40s into a safer two-lane road, and by the mid-1950s, Route 66 was a four-lane expressway. Interstate 15 bypassed the expressway in 1969, but the Route 66 expressway is still there, and it's the perfect place to test Chevrolet Powerglides from the 1950s. Millions of Powerglide-equipped cars climbed the grades in all kinds of weather in the '50s. The highway rose to well over 4,000 elevation, and the grades range from mildly climbing to torturously steep.

The three test vehicles met at approximately 3,000 feet elevation, which was higher than most of these vehicles have been in the time their owners have had them. The elevation was another element in a real world test of three old cars.

The contestants: Ted Taylor and his '51 Deluxe sedan, Bill Quinn and his '53 Bel Air hardtop, and Irv Kushner and his '55 Nomad meet on a closed-off section of Route 66 in California's Cajon Pass for a Powerglide Challenge.

Powerglide

The description of Powerglide's operation in the 1953 *Motor's* repair manual reads exactly the same as the Buick Dynaflow, which was introduced in 1948.

General Motors had brought out the Safety Automatic on Oldsmobiles in 1937, and it was essentially an automatic transmission with fluid coupling that did not shift itself. The Hydra-Matic that came out on Oldsmobiles in 1939 did shift itself, and it was a lot more popular. The Hydra-Matic was a four-speed transmission and, by far, the most advanced and convenient automatic transmission on the road at the time, but the shifts were positive and noticeable, and the non-shifting Dynaflow may have been GM's attempt to counter complaints that the Hydra-Matic was jerky because all Dynaflow advertising stressed how smoothly the transmission operated.

What is a torque converter? Picture the flywheel spinning on the back of the engine. Attach a doughnut-shaped tank full of liquid to it with paddles on the inside—the *impeller*. Picture another set of paddles on the inside of the tank that are attached to a shaft going out the back of the tank and into the transmission gear box—the *turbine*. The engine accelerates, the liquid in the tank flies to the outside under centrifugal force from the impeller, the current grabs the paddles of the turbine, and the car starts to move. There's a period of time when the impeller is outrunning the turbine because of the resistance of getting the car to move, and this is called *slipping*. Once the car is moving pretty good, and the turbine catches up to the impeller, both pieces of the unit are moving at about the same speed without much slipping going on. When the car comes back down to a stop, the centrifugal force decreases, and the engine is able to remain idling after the car has stopped. This two-element system is called a fluid coupling.

The most famous fluid coupling setup was Chrysler's Fluid Drive which, beginning in 1939, put a system like this in front of a three-speed manual transmission. Some people would leave the Chrysler transmission in third gear and just drive around without shifting, but acceleration was slow and gas mileage was poor. Most Chrysler drivers would shift manually between second and third gear with Fluid Drive providing ultra-smooth gear changes. Chrysler added various types of self-shifting gearboxes behind the Fluid Drive unit that required the driver to let off the gas to allow the automatic shift, and

by 1949 this system could be had on a Dodge under the name Gyromatic.

A true torque converter added a few more elements to the fluid coupling concept. In between the impeller and the turbine were two and sometimes three more sets of paddles attached with one-way clutches to concentric shafts leading into the transmission gearbox. These middle elements were sometimes called the *stator* and *secondary stator*. The Dynaflow and Powerglide torque converters evolved quickly through the early-1950s, and the configuration of these elements changed almost yearly. Essentially, the stator and secondary stator would capture the violent currents and shock waves generated in the fluid during the slipping phase of acceleration, capturing the currents and redirecting them in to add force to the forward motion of the car.

Dynaflow did not shift. When the gearshift was put into the "Drive" position, the planetary gearbox engaged in a 1-to-1 ratio, meaning the input shaft from torque converter and the output shaft leading to the differential are turning the same speed. All changes in ratio were accomplished in the torque converter alone. There was also "Low" position on the gearshift that geared down the transmission. The Low position existed mostly to keep the car under control when descending mountain roads, although, many people got into the habit of using the Low gear for quicker acceleration from a standing start.

Chevrolet introduced Powerglide in 1950, and for the first four years, it worked just like Dynaflow, but in 1953, GM installed a valve body in the transmission so the gearbox would shift automatically from Low to Drive, and Powerglide became a true modern automatic transmission that equaled Ford's existing Ford-O-Matic and Chrysler's Powerflite, which also debuted in 1953.

The Contestants

The three contestants are not new cars, trophy-winning trailer queens or modernized resto-rods. These are three used cars in various states of restoration, and they represent Chevrolets in the real world, both as they were when they were several years old and climbing the Cajon Pass and as they are when collectors buy them to drive as daily transportation in addition to being collectible toys.

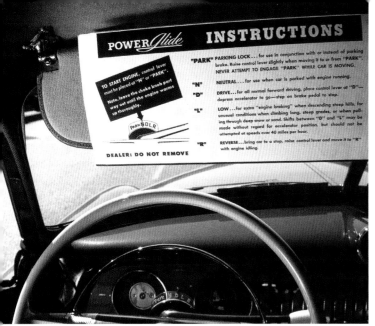

Ted Taylor's 1951 Chevrolet Deluxe sedan was his worn and weathered daily driver for many years before finally being given a long break for restoration. Its rebuilt 235 is a strong engine, but an unforeseen repair caused the installation of a 1958 cylinder head with a slightly higher compression ratio. It may have a little more power than it had when new in 1951, but being tested on a grade at 3,000 feet with two grown men in the cab probably undoes the advantages of the higher compression ratio easily. With engine work having been very common in the 1950s, a '51 Chevrolet with a '58 cylinder head was certainly a common enough sight. Taylor's car represents the six-cylinder, non-shifting Powerglide Chevrolet.

Bill Quinn's 1953 Chevrolet Bel Air two-door hardtop is a pretty car with chrome bows across the headliner and a stylish continental spare on the back. Quinn's Chevrolet is complete and in original condition, but it's also a rather loose, worn car with slack in the power steering, a few rattles, carburetor mixture that was not prepared for such high elevation, and an out-of-adjustment throttle pressure adjustment on the Powerglide. Quinn is dedicated to restoring this worthwhile Chevrolet, and its condition actually helps the test because it's important to remember Chevrolets were economy cars in 1953, and even the most impressive '53 Chevrolet was obsolete by the late 1950s. Many of them climbed the Cajon Pass in this condition in the 1950s, and as Quinn progresses with the restoration, this car will again climb the grades with ease. Quinn's car represents the six-cylinder, shifting Powerglide Chevrolet.

Irv Kushner's 1955 Chevrolet Nomad station wagon is a freshly restored car. The restoration is so recent, in fact, that the rebuilt 265 V-8 isn't quite broken-in or tuned-up completely. The sporty Nomad is loaded with power steering, power brakes and factory air-conditioning. The 265 created the hottest Chevrolet built up to 1955, but it was a small engine compared to what some expensive cars had at the time, and the Nomad's factory weight is a couple of hundred pounds heavier than a 1955 Chevrolet

sedan. Additionally, this Nomad is in the real world with the old-fashioned air-conditioning, a full tank of gas, a battery, and two grown men riding in it adding considerable weight. With breaking-in and tuning-up, Kushner's Nomad will grow more lionhearted, and it represents the V-8 Powerglide Chevrolet.

The Challenge

Unlike most so-called performance tests in car magazines, these cars were tested on a substantial grade from a standing stop with surprising results. The grade was not the steepest the old highway up the Cajon Pass served up, but the cars were definitely driving uphill with less oxygen than they usually have a lower elevations. With the grade working against them, an acceleration test up to 45 mph seemed fair with time being the factor, rather than distance.

The 1951 Chevrolet with the non-shifting Powerglide took off. Taylor was reluctant to leave it in Drive from a standing stop, feeling that it would have been a bit of a strain on the car. He did what a lot of people did with these cars when they were new—pull the Powerglide into Low manually, run the car up to about 25 mph and shifting manually into Drive. The car hit 45 mph against the grade in 20 seconds. The engine was smooth and quiet.

The 1953 Chevrolet took off with its shifting Powerglide. Quinn had to hold the out-of-adjustment Powerglide in Low just as Taylor had, but Quinn shifted the transmission into Drive at the same 25 mph, which is about when it would have shifted automatically anyway, hitting 45 mph in 25 seconds. The car coughed at the high elevation, but with a tune-up and probably a fuel pressure test resulting in a fuel system repair of some kind, the '53 would have at least equaled the '51.

The 1955 Chevrolet Nomad took off with its V-8 and shifting Powerglide. The fresh engine hummed strongly against the grade and pulled the heavier-than-average '55 Chevrolet up to 45 mph in the same 25 seconds it took Quinn's '53.

The 1951 six-cylinder non-shifting Powerglide Chevrolet won the test, but by having been held in Low, it cheated a little. If the '51 had gone from a standing stop in Drive, it's likely that it would have hit 45 mph several seconds later—very close to where the worn '53 and the heavy '55 hit it.

In the real world with real-world disadvantages and in the varying conditions they would have been in as used cars in the late-1950s and early-1960s, they performed equally.

In the mid-1950s, Chevrolet called its V-8 cars the "Hot Ones," and this test does not mean the Hot Ones weren't hot. The 1955 V-8 was only 265 cubic inches, and it certainly did not have the power of the 283s, 327s and 350s the small-block Chevrolet engine grew to in later years. The 265 certainly seemed quicker than the '54 Chevrolet six when they were new, but that wasn't their most noticeable advantage. The V-8 Nomad may not have outrun the other two by much, but it reached highway speed more smoothly, quietly and with much less feeling of effort. Freeways were crossing the U.S. quickly in the 1950s, and this stretch of Route 66 was completed as an expressway in 1955, just in time for Chevrolet's new V-8 to be ready to pull the grades at higher speeds because they would not have been stuck behind trucks nearly as much. The 265 may not win a drag race, but it was certainly more prepared to cruise at higher speeds for sustained periods than the six-cylinder cars.

Other Challenges

The 1951 non-shifting Powerglide Chevrolet is smooth and quiet, and when it's time to take the car through an S-curve at highway speed, it's easy to keep on the road even on bias-ply tires.

The 1953 Bel Air is unsure through the curves in its present condition, but with restoration, it may have an advantage over the '51 because it's a much lower-profile car, and its power steering might not transmit the pavement variations to the driver.

The Nomad uses its weight to stay flat and sure through the curves.

All three cars were pleasant at highway speed, and certainly, the '51 Powerglide-equipped Chevrolet was more roadable than a '51 standard-shift Chevrolet would be in the same situation with its splash-oiled 216 whining from the painful 4.11 that held the standard-shift cars back to 1930s performance standards.

The test driver pretended a St. Bernard came loping out onto the highway, and all the three cars swerved easily and stayed under control. When pretending a bouncing ball came out onto the highway that would, no doubt, be followed by a child, the cars stopped straight. The 1955 Chevrolet's power brakes have a little delay to them, but they work well.

As the '53 gets restored and the '55 breaks in, they will surpass the '51. Doing the same test in a couple of years could reverse the results. In good condition, all of them could be used as daily drivers and cross-country highway cars, unlike standard-shift Chevrolets from the 1940s and early 1950s that would need some special care, special routing, and some patience to do the same. None of these cars sit in the garage, and if they take the beatings the Cajon Pass has to offer, they'll come to life on the world's tamer highways.

How Chevrolet's Powerglide helps the happy couple make a smoother (and thriftier) getaway...

Making your early-'50s Chevrolet run on the highway without ruining originality

Rear axle ratio has a bigger effect on the performance of a car than the engine does. Picture two 1965 Chevrolets with Powerglides—one with a 283-cid V-8, the other with a 327. There might be a difference in performance when the pedal is smashed to the floor with the difference measured in fractions of a second, but in ordinary driving, they will be identical from behind the wheel, and really, the driver could not tell the two engines apart. On the other hand, a 10-percent change in rear axle ratio can make or break even the best car.

A standard-shift 1950 Chevrolet takes off from a stop. The driver runs through the gears and settles into high gear at maybe 35. The car accelerates and the engine gets louder, and louder, and louder. The driver really wants to shift into a higher gear, but there isn't one. The Chevrolet six with babbit bearings, dip oiling and a 15-lb. oil pressure gauge is slamming the relatively heavy pistons up and down a long stroke. The driver levels off the acceleration at about 50 mph, and that's about as fast as the Chevrolet was going on this cross-country trip. The car could go faster, but the driver knew there would be a price later.

The 1950 standard shift Chevrolet had a 4.11 rear axle ratio, but a 1950 Chevrolet with Powerglide had a 3.55 ratio. If both cars are going the same speed, the Powerglide car's engine is revving 15-percent lower in rpm, and it's noticeable from behind the wheel. Indeed, a 15-percent difference in rear axle ratio is the difference between a 50-mph car and a 65-mph car.

The Numbers

The numbers in the rear axle ratio only represent fractions of revolutions, but when they're applied to thousands of rpm and millions of total revolutions over time and miles, a fraction of a turn can make a giant difference.

The number in the ratio tells how many times the engine turns for every one turn of the rear wheels. On a car with a 4.11:1 rear end, the engine turns 4.11 times for every one turn of the rear wheels. In casual conversations, this ratio is pronounced "four-eleven."

Two 1950 Chevrolets leave on a 100-mile trip. One is a standard-shift car with a 4.11 rear end, and the other is a Powerglide-equipped car with a 3.55 rear end. How big a difference does only a half turn of the engine for every one turn of the wheels make? At 60 mph, the standard-shift/4.11 car's engine would be revving 2950 rpm, but the Powerglide/3.55 car's engine would only be revving 2537 rpm. This is a significant difference, and remember, this difference repeats for every minute of driving. Every mile these cars drive, the 3.55 car's engine turns 413 fewer times, meaning that at the end of the 100-mile trip, the Powerglide car's engine would have turned 41,300 fewer times! This is only over the course of 100 miles. Over the course of 10,000 miles of driving, the 3.55 car's engine would have turned over 4.1 million fewer times!

While driving, the 3.55 car is smoother, quieter, and gets better fuel mileage, while the 4.11 car's engine takes a beating as the pistons get slammed from the top to the bottom of the long stroke with great speed and violence which puts a great strain on the babbit rod bearings. Over the long term, the 3.55 car's engine will take much less of a beating because the pistons are not being slammed up and down so fast and hard, and the great reduction in the total number of revs will greatly increase the life of everything from the engine bearings to the water pump.

By the 1960s, the 3.08 rear axle ratio was extremely common on Chevrolets of all sizes and with all engines. The result was an engine that loafed along at around 2200 rpm on cars with 15-inch wheels, and over the same 100-mile trip turned 73,000 fewer times than the 1950 Chevrolet with the 4.11 rear end.

In the Real World

Many old cars have fine drive trains and excellent engineering, and many cars dating clear back to the 1930s are all set for daily and long-distance driving just as they were when they were new. But the cars are also hamstrung by low-geared rear ends that were required for the poor roads of the time. Many cars never saw pavement and spent their entire lives on dirt roads, gravel and mud. Even if a car was lucky enough to find a paved highway, every big truck had a mile of cars stacked behind it at 30 mph up every grade, and the car companies wanted the cars' engines to spin freely at low speeds to prevent overheating and poor fuel economy. Many companies, Chrysler in particular, installed overdrives on their cars in the 1930s, so when a car finally found a good highway, the overdrive handle was pushed into the dash, and the rpm dropped as the car eased up to 65 mph and got 23 mpg.

Low-geared rear ends are one reason some car owners rarely take their antique cars out on today's highways, but the good news is that for many cars, rear ends from the same brand of car but from different years can be harmlessly retrofitted into older cars with no injury to originality or historical accuracy. A *non-altering* change to rear axle ratio can preserve an old-fashioned engine by lowering the number of revs by millions over time. In many cases, the different rear end is of exactly the same design, and the only difference is a different number of teeth on the gears inside.

The Torque Tube (aka, Enclosed Driveshaft)

Most people who've worked on cars since 1950 are used to looking at the bottom of a car and seeing the driveshaft out in the open with two universal joints on each end. This wasn't always the case. Sand and mud were the enemies of early motoring, and many cars had the driveshaft enclosed within a tube running between the transmission and the rear end. By the late-1920s, some companies were getting rid of the enclosed driveshaft and adopting the open system. Ford kept the enclosed driveshaft through 1948, and Chevrolet kept it through 1954, long after most other companies, including other GM divisions, had gotten rid of the awkward system.

The driveshaft enclosure was also called a *torque tube* because, in some cars, the rear axle was supported on coil springs, and the rear end literally pushed the car down the road by the tube around the driveshaft. Buick and Rambler kept enclosed driveshafts into the 1960s.

The torque tube is nothing to fear for the Chevrolet novice. The Chevy system was much easier to work on than Ford's. Clear through 1948, if a mechanic needed to

work on a Ford clutch, he had to either remove the engine, or take the rear end loose and slide it back to pull the torque tube back from the transmission. The Chevrolet was more thought-out, and the torque tube on an early-1950s Chevrolet can be taken loose from the transmission and dropped downward without removing the rear end or moving the engine and transmission forward.

Cars with open driveshafts have a U-joint at each end, and the two allow the rear axle to move up and down as the car encounters uneven pavement. The Chevrolet only has one U-joint at the front, and the driveshaft just fits into the differential on splines and forms a solid connection.

The torque tube bulges outward where it goes into the transmission, and it looks like a ball in a socket. Chevrolet appropriately named it the *torque ball*. If the Chevrolet owner needs to replace the U-joint, for example, he removes the collar around the torque ball from the transmission, loosens the U-joint, and drops the torque tube down from the transmission. The torque ball collar has a seal around it and a gasket where the collar bolts to the transmission, and all of these gaskets and seals are easily available through vintage Chevrolet parts companies.

Changing the Rear Axle Ratio

Most vintage Chevrolet enthusiasts consider installation of a Powerglide rear end into a standard-shift early-1950s Chevrolet to be a non-altering change. The components are identical, and the historical record is intact when the job is done. It may even help cars to stay original by not burning up correct dip-oiled, babbit-bearing, six-cylinder engines at highway speed.

On cars with open driveshafts, once the driveshaft is removed, the axles can be pulled out, and the differential can be dropped out of the rear axle housing and be replaced. On other cars, the whole axle can be replaced.

When Chevrolet restorers talk about the "rear end" on a pre-1955 Chevrolet, they're talking about everything from the torque ball rearward to the differential. The driveshaft, torque tube and differential are thought of as being one piece, and while the piece is large and heavy, replacing it is not hard. The restorer removes the rear brakes, takes the axles loose and pulls them outward from the differential, takes the torque ball lose from the transmission, undoes the U-joint, unbolts the differential from the rear axle housing, and drops the whole unit out of the car. The details are in the pages of Chevrolet shop manuals.

The result is a standard-shift early-1950s Chevrolet that cruises along with much less effort and rpm and a very happy engine destined to live a long life.

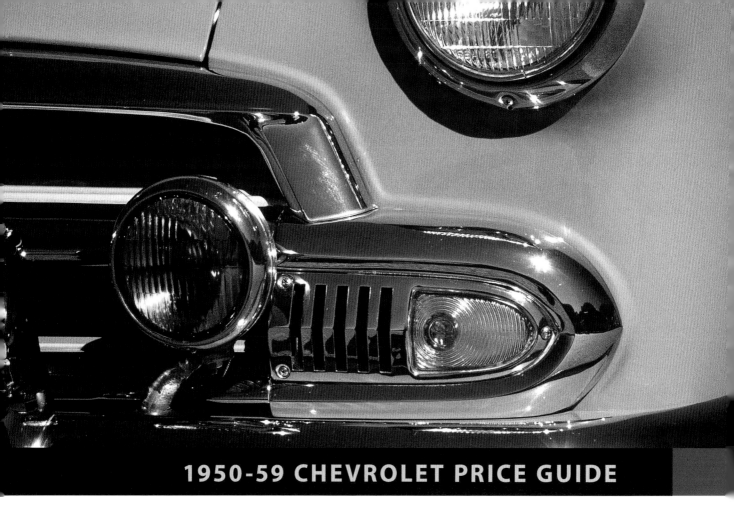

1950-59 CHEVROLET PRICE GUIDE

Vehicle Condition Scale

1. **Excellent.** Restored to current maximum professional standards of quality in every area or perfect original with components operating and appearing as new. A 95-plus point show car that is not driven.

2. **Fine.** Well-restored or a combination of superior restoration and excellent original parts. An extremely well-maintained original vehicle showing minimal wear.

3. **Very good.** Completely operable original or older restoration. A good amateur restoration, or a combination of well-done restoration and good operable components or partially restored car with parts necessary to complete and/or valuable NOS parts.

4. **Good.** A driveable vehicle needing no work or only minor work to be functional. A deteriorated restoration or poor amateur restoration. All components may need restoration to be "excellent" but the car is useable "as is."

5. **Restorable.** Needs complete restoration of body, chassis, and interior. May or may not be running. Isn't weathered or stripped to the point of being useful only for parts.

6. **Parts car.** May or may not be running but is weathered, wrecked and/or stripped to the point of being useful primarily for parts.

1950	6	5	4	3	2	1
1950 Styleline Special, 6-cyl.						
2d Bus Cpe	760	2,280	3,800	8,550	13,300	19,000
2d Spt Cpe	780	2,340	3,900	8,780	13,650	19,500
2d Sed	724	2,172	3,620	8,150	12,670	18,100
4d Sed	728	2,184	3,640	8,190	12,740	18,200

1950 Fleetline Special, 6-cyl.

	6	5	4	3	2	1
2d Sed	728	2,184	3,640	8,190	12,740	18,200
4d Sed	732	2,196	3,660	8,240	12,810	18,300

1950 Styleline DeLuxe, 6-cyl.

	6	5	4	3	2	1
Spt Cpe	800	2,400	4,000	9,000	14,000	20,000
2d Sed	732	2,196	3,660	8,240	12,810	18,300
4d Sed	736	2,208	3,680	8,280	12,880	18,400
2d HT Bel Air (1950 only)	1,020	3,060	5,100	11,480	17,850	25,500
2d Conv	1,520	4,560	7,600	17,100	26,600	38,000
4d Woodie Wag (1949 only)	1,240	3,720	6,200	13,950	21,700	31,000
4d Mtl Sta Wag	920	2,760	4,600	10,350	16,100	23,000

1950 Fleetline DeLuxe, 6-cyl.

	6	5	4	3	2	1
2d Sed	776	2,328	3,880	8,730	13,580	19,400
4d Sed	780	2,340	3,900	8,780	13,650	19,500

1951-52

	6	5	4	3	2	1

1951-52 Styleline Special, 6-cyl.

	6	5	4	3	2	1
2d Bus Cpe	780	2,340	3,900	8,780	13,650	19,500
2d Spt Cpe	788	2,364	3,940	8,870	13,790	19,700
2d Sed	732	2,196	3,660	8,240	12,810	18,300
4d Sed	728	2,184	3,640	8,190	12,740	18,200

1951-52 Styleline DeLuxe, 6-cyl.

	6	5	4	3	2	1
2d Spt Cpe	840	2,520	4,200	9,450	14,700	21,000
2d Sed	752	2,256	3,760	8,460	13,160	18,800
4d Sed	752	2,256	3,760	8,460	13,160	18,800
2d HT Bel Air	1,000	3,000	5,000	11,250	17,500	25,000
2d Conv	1,560	4,680	7,800	17,550	27,300	39,000

1951-52 Fleetline Special, 6-cyl.

	6	5	4	3	2	1
2d Sed	696	2,088	3,480	7,830	12,180	17,400
4d Sed (1951 only)	692	2,076	3,460	7,790	12,110	17,300
4d Sta Wag	800	2,400	4,000	9,000	14,000	20,000

1951-52 Fleetline DeLuxe, 6-cyl.

	6	5	4	3	2	1
2d Sed	764	2,292	3,820	8,600	13,370	19,100
4d Sed (1951 only)	760	2,280	3,800	8,550	13,300	19,000

1953

	6	5	4	3	2	1

1953 Special 150, 6-cyl.

	6	5	4	3	2	1
2d Bus Cpe	720	2,160	3,600	8,100	12,600	18,000
2d Clb Cpe	732	2,196	3,660	8,240	12,810	18,300
2d Sed	688	2,064	3,440	7,740	12,040	17,200
4d Sed	684	2,052	3,420	7,700	11,970	17,100
4d Sta Wag	800	2,400	4,000	9,000	14,000	20,000

1953 DeLuxe 210, 6-cyl.

2d Clb Cpe	800	2,400	4,000	9,000	14,000	20,000
2d Sed	740	2,220	3,700	8,330	12,950	18,500
4d Sed	736	2,208	3,680	8,280	12,880	18,400
2d HT	1,040	3,120	5,200	11,700	18,200	26,000
2d Conv	1,600	4,800	8,000	18,000	28,000	40,000
4d Sta Wag	820	2,460	4,100	9,230	14,350	20,500
4d 210 Townsman Sta Wag	840	2,520	4,200	9,450	14,700	21,000

1953 Bel Air

2d Sed	784	2,352	3,920	8,820	13,720	19,600
4d Sed	780	2,340	3,900	8,780	13,650	19,500
2d HT	1,080	3,240	5,400	12,150	18,900	27,000
2d Conv	1,720	5,160	8,600	19,350	30,100	43,000

1953 Corvette

6-cyl. Conv	4,800	14,400	24,000	54,000	84,000	120,000

1954

	6	5	4	3	2	1

1954 Special 150, 6-cyl.

2d Utl Sed	680	2,040	3,400	7,650	11,900	17,000
2d Sed	688	2,064	3,440	7,740	12,040	17,200
4d Sed	684	2,052	3,420	7,700	11,970	17,100
4d Sta Wag	800	2,400	4,000	9,000	14,000	20,000

1954 Special 210, 6-cyl.

2d Sed	740	2,220	3,700	8,330	12,950	18,500
2d Sed Delray	800	2,400	4,000	9,000	14,000	20,000
4d Sed	736	2,208	3,680	8,280	12,880	18,400
4d Sta Wag	840	2,520	4,200	9,450	14,700	21,000

1954 Bel Air, 6-cyl.

2d Sed	788	2,364	3,940	8,870	13,790	19,700
4d Sed	784	2,352	3,920	8,820	13,720	19,600
2d HT	1,080	3,240	5,400	12,150	18,900	27,000
2d Conv	1,760	5,280	8,800	19,800	30,800	44,000
4d Sta Wag	920	2,760	4,600	10,350	16,100	23,000

1954 Corvette

6-cyl. Conv	3,000	9,000	15,000	33,750	52,500	75,000

1955

	1	2	3	4	5	6

1955 Model 150, V-8

2d Utl Sed	720	2,160	3,600	8,100	12,600	18,000
2d Sed	800	2,400	4,000	9,000	14,000	20,000
4d Sed	720	2,160	3,600	8,100	12,600	18,000

	6	5	4	3	2	1
4d Sta Wag	760	2,280	3,800	8,550	13,300	19,000

1955 Model 210, V-8

	6	5	4	3	2	1
2d Sed	840	2,520	4,200	9,450	14,700	21,000
2d Sed Delray	880	2,640	4,400	9,900	15,400	22,000
4d Sed	720	2,160	3,600	8,100	12,600	18,000
2d HT	1,280	3,840	6,400	14,400	22,400	32,000
2d Sta Wag	820	2,460	4,100	9,230	14,350	20,500
4d Sta Wag	780	2,340	3,900	8,780	13,650	19,500

1955 Bel Air, V-8

	6	5	4	3	2	1
2d Sed	880	2,640	4,400	9,900	15,400	22,000
4d Sed	800	2,400	4,000	9,000	14,000	20,000
2d HT	1,440	4,320	7,200	16,200	25,200	36,000
2d Conv	2,440	7,320	12,200	27,450	42,700	61,000
2d Nomad	1,480	4,440	7,400	16,650	25,900	37,000
4d Sta Wag	880	2,640	4,400	9,900	15,400	22,000

NOTE: *Add 10 percent for A/C; 15 percent for "Power-Pack". Deduct 10 percent for 6-cyl.*

1955 Corvette

	6	5	4	3	2	1
6-cyl. Conv	3,080	9,240	15,400	34,650	53,900	77,000
8-cyl. Conv	3,200	9,600	16,000	36,000	56,000	80,000

NOTE: *Add $3,000 & up for access. hardtop.*

1956

	6	5	4	3	2	1

1956 Model 150, V-8

	6	5	4	3	2	1
2d Utl Sed	720	2,160	3,600	8,100	12,600	18,000
2d Sed	800	2,400	4,000	9,000	14,000	20,000
4d Sed	720	2,160	3,600	8,100	12,600	18,000
2d Sta Wag	800	2,400	4,000	9,000	14,000	20,000

1956 Model 210, V-8

	6	5	4	3	2	1
2d Sed	840	2,520	4,200	9,450	14,700	21,000
2d Sed Delray	880	2,640	4,400	9,900	15,400	22,000
4d Sed	720	2,160	3,600	8,100	12,600	18,000
4d HT	800	2,400	4,000	9,000	14,000	20,000
2d HT	1,240	3,720	6,200	13,950	21,700	31,000

	6	5	4	3	2	1
2d Sta Wag	840	2,520	4,200	9,450	14,700	21,000
4d Sta Wag	760	2,280	3,800	8,550	13,300	19,000
4d 9P Sta Wag	780	2,340	3,900	8,780	13,650	19,500

1956 Bel Air, V-8

	6	5	4	3	2	1
2d Sed	880	2,640	4,400	9,900	15,400	22,000
4d Sed	800	2,400	4,000	9,000	14,000	20,000
4d HT	840	2,520	4,200	9,450	14,700	21,000
2d HT	1,400	4,200	7,000	15,750	24,500	35,000
2d Conv	2,400	7,200	12,000	27,000	42,000	60,000
2d Nomad	1,440	4,320	7,200	16,200	25,200	36,000
4d 9P Sta Wag	880	2,640	4,400	9,900	15,400	22,000

NOTE: *Add 10 percent for A/C; 15 percent for "Power-Pack". Deduct 10 percent for 6-cyl. Add 25 percent for dual 4 barrel carbs.*

1956 Corvette

	6	5	4	3	2	1
Conv	3,040	9,120	15,200	34,200	53,200	76,000

NOTE: *All post-1955 Corvettes are V-8 powered. Add $3,000 & up for removable hardtop. Add 20 percent for two 4 barrel carbs.*

1957	6	5	4	3	2	1

1957 Model 150, V-8

	6	5	4	3	2	1
2d Utl Sed	760	2,280	3,800	8,550	13,300	19,000
2d Sed	840	2,520	4,200	9,450	14,700	21,000
4d Sed	740	2,220	3,700	8,330	12,950	18,500
2d Sta Wag	820	2,460	4,100	9,230	14,350	20,500

1957 Model 210, V-8

	6	5	4	3	2	1
2d Sed	880	2,640	4,400	9,900	15,400	22,000
2d Sed Delray	920	2,760	4,600	10,350	16,100	23,000
4d Sed	820	2,460	4,100	9,230	14,350	20,500
4d HT	880	2,640	4,400	9,900	15,400	22,000
2d HT	1,280	3,840	6,400	14,400	22,400	32,000
2d Sta Wag	880	2,640	4,400	9,900	15,400	22,000
4d Sta Wag	800	2,400	4,000	9,000	14,000	20,000

	6	5	4	3	2	1
4d 9P Sta Wag	820	2,460	4,100	9,230	14,350	20,500

1957 Bel Air, V-8

2d Sed	920	2,760	4,600	10,350	16,100	23,000
4d Sed	820	2,460	4,100	9,230	14,350	20,500
4d HT	880	2,640	4,400	9,900	15,400	22,000
2d HT	1,480	4,440	7,400	16,650	25,900	37,000
2d Conv	2,520	7,560	12,600	28,350	44,100	63,000
2d Nomad	1,560	4,680	7,800	17,550	27,300	39,000
4d Sta Wag	920	2,760	4,600	10,350	16,100	23,000

NOTE: *Add 10 percent for A/C; 15 percent for "Power-Pack" and 20 percent for F.I. Deduct 10 percent for 6-cyl. Add 25 percent for dual 4 barrel carbs.*

1957 Corvette

Conv	3,080	9,240	15,400	34,650	53,900	77,000

NOTE: *Add $3,000 for hardtop. Add 50 percent for F.I., 250 hp. Add 75 percent for F.I., 283 hp. Add 25 percent for two 4 barrel carbs, 245 hp. Add 35 percent for two 4 barrel carbs, 270 hp. Add 15 percent for 4-speed transmission. Add 150 percent for 579E option.*

1958

	6	5	4	3	2	1

1958 Delray, V-8

2d Utl Sed	680	2,040	3,400	7,650	11,900	17,000
2d Sed	700	2,100	3,500	7,880	12,250	17,500
4d Sed	660	1,980	3,300	7,430	11,550	16,500

1958 Biscayne, V-8

2d Sed	680	2,040	3,400	7,650	11,900	17,000
4d Sed	664	1,992	3,320	7,470	11,620	16,600

1958 Bel Air, V-8

2d Sed	760	2,280	3,800	8,550	13,300	19,000
4d Sed	740	2,220	3,700	8,330	12,950	18,500
4d HT	800	2,400	4,000	9,000	14,000	20,000
2d HT	920	2,760	4,600	10,350	16,100	23,000
2d Impala	1,640	4,920	8,200	18,450	28,700	41,000
2d Imp Conv	2,400	7,200	12,000	27,000	42,000	60,000

1958 Station Wagons, V-8

2d Yeo	744	2,232	3,720	8,370	13,020	18,600
4d Yeo	740	2,220	3,700	8,330	12,950	18,500
4d 6P Brookwood	752	2,256	3,760	8,460	13,160	18,800
4d 9P Brookwood	756	2,268	3,780	8,510	13,230	18,900
4d Nomad	820	2,460	4,100	9,230	14,350	20,500

NOTE: *Add 10 percent for "Power-Pack" & dual exhaust on 283 V-8. Add 20 percent for 348. Add 30 percent for 348 Tri-Power set up. Add 15 percent for A/C. Deduct 10 percent for 6-cyl.*

1958 Corvette

Conv	2,640	7,920	13,200	29,700	46,200	66,000

NOTE: *Add $3,000 for hardtop. Add 25 percent for two 4 barrel carbs, 245 hp. Add 35 percent for two 4 barrel carbs, 270 hp. Add 40 percent for F.I., 250 hp. Add 60 percent for F.I., 290 hp.*

1959	6	5	4	3	2	1

1959 Biscayne, V-8

	6	5	4	3	2	1
2d Utl Sed	640	1,920	3,200	7,200	11,200	16,000
2d Sed	652	1,956	3,260	7,340	11,410	16,300
4d Sed	648	1,944	3,240	7,290	11,340	16,200

1959 Bel Air, V-8

2d Sed	672	2,016	3,360	7,560	11,760	16,800
4d Sed	668	2,004	3,340	7,520	11,690	16,700
4d HT	720	2,160	3,600	8,100	12,600	18,000

1959 Impala, V-8

4d Sed	680	2,040	3,400	7,650	11,900	17,000
4d HT	760	2,280	3,800	8,550	13,300	19,000
2d HT	1,120	3,360	5,600	12,600	19,600	28,000
2d Conv	1,640	4,920	8,200	18,450	28,700	41,000

1959 Station Wagons, V-8

2d Brookwood	720	2,160	3,600	8,100	12,600	18,000
4d Brookwood	680	2,040	3,400	7,650	11,900	17,000
4d Parkwood	696	2,088	3,480	7,830	12,180	17,400
4d Kingswood	720	2,160	3,600	8,100	12,600	18,000
4d Nomad	740	2,220	3,700	8,330	12,950	18,500

NOTE: *Add 10 percent for A/C. Add 5 percent for 4-speed transmission. Deduct 10 percent for 6-cyl. Add 30 percent for 348 Tri-Power setup.*

1959 Corvette

Conv	2,280	6,840	11,400	25,650	39,900	57,000

NOTE: *Add $3,000 for hardtop. Add 40 percent for F.I., 250 hp. Add 60 percent for F.I., 290 hp. Add 25 percent for two 4 barrel carbs, 245 hp. Add 35 percent for two 4 barrel carbs, 270 hp.*